Don't Lose Your Crown

by Warren W. Wiersbe
General Director
Back to the Bible Broadcast

A
BACK TO THE BIBLE
PUBLICATION
LINCOLN, NE. 68501

VICTOR
BOOKS a division of SP Publications, Inc.
WHEATON ILLINOIS 60187

Offices also in
Whitby, Ontario, Canada
Amersham-on-the-Hill, Bucks, England

84,000 printed to date—1985
(5-3513—65M—25)
ISBN 0-8474-6511-X

All Scripture quotations are from *The New Scofield Reference Bible.*

Printed in the United States of America

Contents

Chapter 1

The Cry for a King
(I Sam. 8)

The life of Saul, the first king of Israel, is a study in contrasts. Saul began his reign in victory, and he ended it in humiliating defeat. He lost his character, his power and, ultimately, his crown and his life. King Saul stands as a warning to all of us that no matter what our station in life may be, we cannot rebel against God and get away with it. Revelation 3:11 says it perfectly, "Behold, I come quickly: hold that fast which thou hast, that no man take thy crown." Paul warned us in I Corinthians 10:12, "Wherefore let him that thinketh he standeth take heed lest he fall." What a tragedy it is to fall and to lose your crown!

Saul's story begins with Israel's cry for a king: "And it came to pass, when Samuel was old, that he made his sons judges over Israel. . . . And his sons walked not in his ways, but turned aside after money, and took bribes, and perverted justice. Then all the elders of Israel gathered themselves together, and came to Samuel unto Ramah, and said unto him, Behold, thou art old, and thy sons

5

walk not in thy ways; now make us a king to judge us like all the nations. But the thing displeased Samuel, when they said, Give us a king to judge us. And Samuel prayed unto the Lord. And the Lord said unto Samuel, Hearken unto the voice of the people in all that they say unto thee; for they have not rejected thee, but they have rejected me, that I should not reign over them" (I Sam. 8:1,3-7).

When you look at this event, you can well understand why the people wanted a king. I am not saying that their decision was right, but I can understand their reasoning. When you read I Samuel 8, you discover a number of reasons why the people wanted a king. They were human reasons, but behind the human reasons were also divine reasons because God was in control of the situation. God is always in control of every situation. The Bible teaches both divine sovereignty and human responsibility. We can't fully understand it, nor can we explain it; but we believe it because it's taught in the Word of God. When God cannot rule because of the stubbornness of people, He overrules and accomplishes His divine purposes.

Human Reasons

Looking at this event from a human point of view, let's consider a number of reasons why the people wanted a king. To begin with, there was *internal division*. We read in the Book of Judges: "In those days there was no king in Israel, but every man did that which was right in his own eyes" (17:6;21:25). According to the history recorded in Judges, the

6

nation of Israel was not really much of a "nation." It was more like a loose confederation of tribes. The tabernacle held them together, as did the prophets and judges; but when it came to merging all of these tribes into one nation, they never quite accomplished it in the period of the judges. The situation in Israel at that time was similar to the situation in the United States of America when we had the Articles of Confederation—before the Constitution was written. The individual states were loosely organized; each state had its own currency and its own system of government. There was really very little unity.

It is dangerous to be so loosely organized because, when the enemy attacks, you need to be united. There is also the danger of internal power struggles— one tribe wants to have more authority than another tribe. When the elders of Israel saw internal chaos in the nation, they said, "We must have a king." In looking back at this event, you and I say, "Well, they *did* have a king! God was their king! If they had only bowed down to Him and obeyed Him, they would have had unity, prosperity and blessing!" But, alas, every man did what was right in his own eyes.

A second reason why they asked for a king was because of *external danger*. First Samuel 12:12 says, "And when ye saw that Nahash, the king of the children of Ammon, came against you, ye said unto me [Samuel], Nay, but a king shall reign over us; when the Lord your God was your king." The enemy, the Ammonites, was about to attack, and

7

those loosely confederated tribes could not go out and fight such a well-organized army. Later on, the Philistines showed up to create further problems (ch. 13). With the enemy on the outside and division on the inside, the leaders of Israel realized that they needed some kind of unity. We can well appreciate their concern.

A third reason they wanted a king was because of *leadership decay*. Samuel's sons were not walking in the way of their father (8:1-5). They were accepting bribes and perverting justice, and their only purpose in serving was to make money. It's really unfortunate when the second or third generation tears down what their fathers built! This tragedy also happened with Eli's sons (2:12—3:18). Eli, the high priest, should have raised his sons to walk in the ways of the Lord. Because he didn't, Samuel deposed him, and now Samuel himself was going to be deposed for the very same reason! Once again we remember Paul's warning in I Corinthians 10:12: "Wherefore, let him that thinketh he standeth take heed lest he fall."

One of our greatest obligations as Christians is to raise our children to know the Lord. It's a wonderful thing for pastors and missionaries, Sunday school teachers and deacons, elders and trustees to be helping others and to be witnessing and working in the church. But if we lose our own children, what have we gained? If we don't lead our own children to the Lord and challenge them to follow Him, what will happen to God's Church in the future? The Church is only one generation away from extinc-

8

tion. For some reason, Samuel was not able to raise his sons to be good judges—men who were honest, trustworthy, obedient and spiritual. It has well been said that the first generation wins the battle, the second generation claims the spoils, and the third generation wastes it all and goes back into the hands of the enemy.

The nation faced external danger, internal division and leadership decay. I think the elders of Israel were also afraid that Samuel would set up a family dynasty. His godless sons would take over, and then his grandsons would rule. There was no guarantee that the next generation would be spiritual. However, when you consider the kingship in Israel, there was no guarantee of family success. Sometimes one king was a godly man, while his son was ungodly. Ungodly Ahaz was the father of godly Hezekiah, and Hezekiah was the father of ungodly Manasseh! The sons of the godly kings were not always godly.

Likewise, you cannot guarantee a "spiritual dynasty" in your family. No one can guarantee that the next generation will be spiritual. You can do your best to raise godly children, you can set a good example, and you can pray, but none of these things will guarantee that your sons and daughters will be spiritual. I'm sure Samuel did all these things, but his sons still became prodigals who were not fit to be in places of leadership.

Here then are three human reasons why the Israelites wanted a king: internal division, external danger and leadership decay.

Divine Reasons

Besides the human reasons for wanting a king, God had His own purposes for giving the Israelites a king. God, who sees the heart, always knows what the true motive is. The basic reason for their request was *spiritual declension*. The people were acting in fear and unbelief. They wanted to imitate the other nations. When the other nations went to war, their king guided them. When the nations had their council, the king led them. The Israelites forgot that they were *not* to be like other nations. Even Balaam, as wicked as he was, knew that Israel was a special nation. "Lo, the people shall dwell alone, and shall not be reckoned among the nations" (Num. 23:9). No one can treat the nation of Israel the way he treats other nations because the Israelites are God's chosen people. Moses said in Exodus 33:16, "For wherein shall it be known here that I and thy people have found grace in thy sight? Is it not in that thou goest with us? So shall we be separated, I and thy people, from all the people that are upon the face of the earth." Israel's distinction was that it was not to be like the other nations but was to be separated from them and different from them.

"Give us a king!" the elders cried, and Samuel's heart was broken. He prayed about it, because Samuel was a great man of prayer. God said to him, "For they have not rejected thee, but they have rejected me, that I should not reign over them" (I Sam. 8:7). The leaders walked by sight and not by faith. As a result, they rejected God the Father.

10

Centuries later, the nation rejected God the Son: "Crucify him! . . . We have no king but Caesar" (John 19:15). Then they rejected God the Holy Spirit when they stoned Stephen. "Ye stiff-necked and uncircumcised in heart and ears, ye do always resist the Holy Spirit; as your fathers did, so do ye" (Acts 7:51). What an indictment! The Israelites rejected God the Father in the days of Samuel; they rejected God the Son in the days of our Lord Jesus Christ; and they rejected God the Holy Spirit in the days of the apostles. No wonder God had to reject them as a nation!

"Give us a king!" Often in the history of Israel you find the people asking for a substitute for God. When Moses was up on the mountain for a lengthy period, the people cried, "Make us gods" (Ex. 32:1). When they were at Kadesh-barnea and refused to go into the land, they cried, "Let us make a captain, and let us return into Egypt" (Num. 14:4). Israel had the Almighty God as their King and Defender, and yet they wanted a substitute! This was spiritual declension—they did not trust God to protect them.

A fifth reason why God allowed them to have a king was for *divine discipline*. God gave them what they asked for, and they lived to regret it. God responded to their needs out of compassion, but He also responded in discipline. "I have looked upon my people, because their cry is come unto me" (I Sam. 9:16). God was compassionate, but He was also concerned because they were rejecting His

11

leadership. He was not caught off guard but was well aware of their true motives.

When God called Abraham, He told him that kings would come from his loins (see Gen. 17:6,16). So from the beginning of Jewish history, God knew that the nation would produce kings. God told the tribe of Judah that it would be the kingly tribe. Genesis 49:10 says, "The scepter shall not depart from Judah, nor a lawgiver from between his feet, until Shiloh [the Lord Jesus Christ] come." Moses had also predicted the kingship: "When thou art come unto the land which the Lord thy God giveth thee, and shalt possess it, and shalt dwell therein, and shalt say, I will set a king over me, like all the nations that are about me; thou shalt surely set him king over thee whom the Lord thy God shall choose" (Deut. 17:14,15). So God knew the Israelites would ask for a king.

In giving the Israelites a king, God was actually disciplining them. Samuel warned the nation that their king would make difficult demands on them (I Sam. 8), but they insisted that God give them a king. God used that king to discipline them. He gave them their request to teach them not to trust in man but to trust in Him.

What does this mean to us today? Let God be your king. Don't tell Him what to do. If you have disobeyed Him, confess it and trust His grace. God will rule and overrule and accomplish His purposes in your life without your telling Him what to do. If you are not careful about what you pray for, God may grant your request and use it to discipline you.

You need to remember that God knows your needs and will provide for you if you allow Him to be your king: "But seek ye first the kingdom of God, and his righteousness, and all these things shall be added unto you" (Matt. 6:33).

Chapter 2

The People's Choice
(I Sam. 9,10)

In their stubborn rebellion against God, the Israelites asked for a king, and God gave them their request. "I gave thee a king in mine anger, and took him away in my wrath" (Hos. 13:11). God gave them a king not only to meet their needs but also to discipline them. He wanted to teach them some lessons about His own sovereignty and their responsibility.

II Chronicles 20:6 reads: "O Lord God of our fathers, art not thou God in heaven? And rulest not thou over all the kingdoms of the nations? And in thine hand is there not power and might, so that none is able to withstand thee?" In other words, God is sovereign in all the affairs of this world, but man is also responsible. Divine sovereignty and human responsibility are both taught in the Bible, and we must keep them in balance. If you emphasize only divine sovereignty, then you make God responsible for man's sin. If you emphasize only human responsibility, then you rob God of His power and glory. The two go together. The choosing of a king for Israel shows how divine sovereignty and human responsibility work together to accomplish God's purpose on earth. When God is not permitted to rule, then He will overrule. God will accomplish His purpose.

God Calls Saul

In I Samuel 9 we see the human side of Saul (what he was in himself), while in chapter 10 we see God's working in Saul's life (what God did for him). It's important for us to see both aspects in Saul's life.

Let's begin by looking at the man Saul. Notice the natural, positive qualities that apparently made him a good choice for king. God does not bypass our humanity. People have the idea that God invades our humanity and bypasses our human qualities; instead, He *uses* those qualities. God is looking for people whom He can use. He prepares people for the job He has for them. In Psalm 139:13-16 we are told that even our genetic structure, the way we are made physically, is ordained by God. He creates us with particular characteristics because He has certain tasks for each one of us to perform. This was true of Saul. Examine the various qualities he had that would point to great success in his kingship.

"Now there was a man of Benjamin, whose name was Kish, . . . a Benjamite, a mighty man of power" (I Sam. 9:1). First, Saul came from a leading family. The word "power" in this verse means "wealth." The tribe of Benjamin was not a large tribe; in fact, it was one of the smallest. Perhaps it didn't take a great deal of wealth to be a mighty man in the tribe

16

of Benjamin, but at least Saul came from a leading family. His father, Kish, apparently was quite successful, and since Saul was working with his father, he enjoyed the benefits of that success.

Second, he was physically strong and attractive. "And he had a son, whose name was Saul, a choice young man, and handsome; and there was not among the children of Israel a more handsome person than he; from his shoulders and upward he was taller than any of the people" (v. 2). In the East height is very important; those who are tall are respected and admired. Saul was physically strong and attractive. There is nothing wrong with this. Those of us who may not be blessed with great physical strength or with beauty may look down on those who possess it, but we should not. God can use a person's physical characteristics for His service, including the fact that he or she is good looking.

Saul was also obedient to his father. "And the asses of Kish, Saul's father, were lost. And Kish said to Saul, his son, Take now one of the servants with thee, and arise, go seek the asses" (v. 3). This seems like an insignificant event. Some valuable animals are lost, and Saul goes to find them. Yet this insignificant event led to some great things. Little did Saul realize, when he went to look for those animals, that he would meet Samuel, that he would be anointed king and that he would come home the leader of the entire nation of Israel.

We never know what great doors may turn upon small hinges! This was true of David. He was taking

17

care of his father's sheep when his father told him to take some supplies to his brothers in Saul's army. That's when he met Goliath and achieved a great victory.

If you have some insignificant task to perform today, perform it. Do it right. Do the very best you can. It may be the door to some other great responsibility and privilege.

Saul was obedient to his father. He didn't say, "I've got more important things to do. Don't ask me to go out and look for a bunch of animals!" Instead, he obeyed his father and was diligent in pursuing this particular task. He and the servant went through the hill country of Ephraim and then passed through the land of Shalisha. They couldn't find the animals, but they kept on looking. They were diligent. I appreciate people who finish what they start.

Notice in I Samuel 9:5 that Saul had a concern for his father. When they came to the land of Zuph, Saul said to his servant, "Come, and let us return; lest my father leave caring for the asses, and become anxious for us." I appreciate this characteristic in Saul. He was concerned about others. He did not want to cause his father to worry.

These are good character traits, aren't they? Saul came from a leading family, he was physically strong, he was attractive, he was obedient, he was persistent and diligent in doing the job given to him, and he cared about others. He was also willing to listen to counsel. His servant suggested they visit the man of God, Samuel. It doesn't appear that Saul knew who Samuel was before this time. He did not even know that a man of God was there. You get the feeling, as you read these chapters, that King Saul did not have the kind of upbringing that would acquaint him with a man like Samuel. You would think that *everybody* would have known who Samuel was! He was the prophet of God, the great prayer warrior; yet Saul did not know him.

I appreciate the fact that the servant knew Samuel and that he believed Samuel could help. However, it's unfortunate when people turn to God's servant only when they're in trouble. I've pastored three churches, and I've often seen this. Some people don't want you around when things are going well. When you stop to visit them, they don't want you to waste their time. They don't want to come to church or to be bothered by the pastor. But just let trouble enter their home, and they show up in prayer meeting! Just let some difficult problem come into their life, and they instantly come to see the preacher!

Saul and his servant did meet Samuel. First Samuel 9 tells how Samuel took Saul and his servant to dinner. They shared the best part of a big feast because God had told Samuel, in effect, "I'm going to send you the king." Early the next day—at dawn—Samuel walked with Saul to the edge of the city and there anointed him to be king (see 9:26—10:1).

It's interesting that Saul's career as king began at dawn as the sun was coming up. His career ended with the sun going down! At night, Saul disguised himself and went to consult a witch. Then he went

19

out to the battlefield and was slain. All of Saul's good qualities were no guarantee of success.

God Equips Saul

What did God do for Saul? We are told in I Samuel 10. Remember, Saul was God's choice. He was the one God appointed to be the new king. God did it because the people needed a king and also because He was going to teach them some important spiritual lessons. Notice the wonderful assurances that God gave to Saul. One day as I was reading this chapter, I saw these assurances for the first time. I was going through some trying times in my own life and ministry, and I had some important decisions to make. God said to me from this chapter, "Stop worrying! If I have called you, I will equip you." That's what God told Saul in I Samuel 10. In chapter 9 He called Saul, and in chapter 10 He promised to equip him.

In I Samuel 10:2 God assured Saul that He would solve his problems. After Samuel anointed Saul, he assured him that the asses had been found and that he could stop worrying. When the servant of God is in the will of God, God solves the problems. God was saying to Saul, "No matter what problems you face now that you are king, remember that I can solve them."

If you have been called to a place of leadership and yet you are worried or anxious about some situation, remember that God can solve your problems. Just do what He wants you to do.

20

After Samuel anointed Saul, God gave Saul the assurance that He would help him. Then Samuel said, in effect, "Keep going forward, and you will meet three men going to Bethel. They will be carrying three loaves of bread, a skin of wine and three kids. They will greet you and will give you two loaves of bread." Here is the second assurance: *God will supply your needs.* As the new king, Saul would require all kinds of provisions. Samuel assured Saul that God would supply what he needed.

You may be in a building program now. You may be going into a new ministry, wondering where the provisions will come from. They will come from God. The same God who called you will equip you. The One who anointed you will provide what you need.

Samuel gave Saul a third assurance: *God will supply the power that you need.* Samuel told Saul that he would come to the hill of God and would meet some prophets. "And the Spirit of the Lord will come upon thee, and thou shalt prophesy with them, and shalt be turned into another man" (v. 6). God would make a new person out of Saul when the Spirit of God would come upon him. This would transform him from an ordinary farmer into a leader!

In Old Testament times the Spirit of God came upon people temporarily and would sometimes depart from them. This is not true in the New Testament age. Jesus told His disciples that the Spirit of truth would abide with believers forever (see John 14:16). The Spirit will not depart from us; instead,

21

He seals us unto the day of redemption (see Eph. 1:13,14).

When Saul met these prophets, the Spirit of God came upon him, and he became a different person. Saul couldn't become a new person on his own; the work of God's Spirit was needed to change him. "Not by might, nor by power, but by my Spirit, saith the Lord of hosts" (Zech. 4:6).

First Samuel 10:7 records another wonderful assurance from God. "And let it be, when these signs are come unto thee, that thou do as occasion serve thee; for God is with thee." God is with you as you serve Him. Hebrews 13:5 says, "I will never leave thee, nor forsake thee." The same thought is expressed in Matthew 28:20: "Lo, I am with thee always, even unto the end of the age."

A final assurance was given to Saul: "And Saul also went home to Gibeah; and there went with him a band of men, whose hearts God had touched" (I Sam. 10:26). God would provide the people. A king needs people—assistants, servants, soldiers. It was as if God said, "Saul, don't worry about this. I am the One who can provide the people whom you need."

If you are serving the Lord, God will give you all that is needed. He will solve the problems, give necessary provisions, provide His Spirit's power, assure you of His presence and call the right people to help you do the jobs He wants you to do.

When Saul went home, he didn't tell anyone about what had happened. He appears to have been a very modest person. In fact, when Samuel first met him, Saul said, "Am not I a Benjamite, of the smallest of the tribes of Israel, and my family the least of all the families of the tribe of Benjamin?" (9:21). Saul was sincerely humble. When his uncle asked him what had happened, Saul didn't tell him anything about his kingship. He didn't call a press conference! He was humble.

If God calls you, then He will equip you. Trust Him and don't run away from your calling. When they looked for Saul, he was hiding (see 10:22)! G. Campbell Morgan has said, "If God has called a man to kingship, there's no right to hide away." I agree with that. Saul had much going for him. What a pity he turned away from God and failed. "Behold, I come quickly; hold that fast which thou hast, that no man take thy crown" (Rev. 3:11).

Chapter 3

The Conquering Hero
(I Sam. 11,12)

Saul went back to his father's farm in Gibeah and said nothing about the kingship. Life went on as usual until one day when the enemy approached and when the nation of Israel faced a crisis. This was Saul's time of testing. As the new king, he had to help his people. Let's notice the three challenges that Saul had to face and how he responded to them.

The Attack of the Enemy

First Samuel 11:1-11 records the first challenge: *the attack of the enemy.* "Then Nahash the Ammonite, came up, and encamped against Jabesh-gilead; and all the men of Jabesh said unto Nahash, Make a covenant with us, and we will serve thee. And Nahash, the Ammonite, answered them, On this condition will I make a covenant with you, that I may thrust out all your right eyes, and lay it for a reproach upon all Israel. And the elders of Jabesh said unto him, Give us seven days' respite, that we may send messengers unto all the borders of Israel;

25

and then, if there be no man to save us, we will come out to thee. Then came the messengers to Gibeah of Saul, and told the tidings in the hearing of the people; and all the people lifted up their voices, and wept. And, behold, Saul came after the herd out of the field; and Saul said, What aileth the people that they weep? And they told him the tidings of the men of Jabesh. And the Spirit of God came upon Saul when he heard those tidings, and his anger was kindled greatly" (vv. 1-6).

How did the people respond to this crisis? It was a terribly humiliating offer! It would have been bad enough to serve the enemy, but to be disfigured and humiliated as well was just too much. Some of the Israelites said, "Let's wait. Maybe somebody can save us." Others just wept and said, "There's no hope! We're going to have to give up!"

What was Saul's response to this challenge? He assumed his role of leadership and prepared the men for battle. I appreciate his response to this situation. A crisis doesn't make a person; rather, it shows what a person is made of.

Saul was not yet considered a great hero. He had been anointed king, but he had gone back to the farm. Having a monarchy was a brand-new experience for the people of Israel. It seems strange that no one said, "We have a king, so let's go ask him what to do." The monarchy had not yet developed. When the crisis came, Saul met the challenge, solidified the monarchy and proved himself a leader.

Saul's first response was that of righteous indignation. "And the Spirit of God came upon Saul when he heard those tidings, and his anger was kindled greatly" (v. 6). We should have a righteous indignation against the enemies of God. It's very easy for us to say, "We should hate sin but love the sinner." The difficulty comes in separating the sin from the sinner! We may want to deal with the enemy in love, but sometimes we have to declare war. The Spirit of God had changed Saul into another man. He was no longer simply a tall, handsome farmer. Now he was the king, the leader of God's people; and it was time to act.

Saul also received a holy endowment. "And the Spirit of God came upon Saul when he heard those tidings" (v. 6). In chapter 10 we learned that the Holy Spirit of God came upon Saul in great power. Saul was a new man. We cannot fight the battles of God in our own strength. The Spirit of God came upon Saul just as He had upon the judges—people such as Gideon and Samson—and gave him victory.

Saul faced this challenge with faith and courage. "And he took a yoke of oxen, and hewed [cut] them in pieces, and sent them throughout all the borders of Israel" (v. 7). Then he issued a challenge: "Whosoever cometh not forth after Saul and after Samuel, so shall it be done unto his oxen. And the fear of the Lord fell on the people, and they came out with one consent" (v. 7). I like the way Saul openly joined himself with Samuel. You cannot win battles alone; you need others standing with you. Samuel was a great man of prayer, and every leader needs prayer if he is to succeed.

The result of this challenge was the gathering of a

large army. The Children of Israel numbered 300,000, and the men of Judah were 30,000 in number (see v. 8). They united to help the people of Jabesh-gilead. Saul used the same approach Gideon had used: He divided the people into three companies and attacked the enemy in the morning. God gave Israel a great victory. The enemy soldiers were scattered so that not even two of them were left together! (see v. 11).

Saul was challenged by the attack of the enemy. How did he respond? He responded by letting God use him to accomplish the work that needed to be done. God, in turn, equipped him to do the task. This should have been a great encouragement to Saul, for God fulfilled His promises to supply all that Saul needed. This should also be a great encouragement for us. God honored Saul's faith when he was willing to trust Him and fight the enemy, and He will honor our faith when we trust Him and allow Him to work through us.

The Advice of Friends

The second challenge Saul faced occurred after the victory. He had faced the attack of the enemy without too much difficulty, but now he had to face *the advice of his friends*. "And the people said unto Samuel, Who is he that said, Shall Saul reign over us? Bring the men, that we may put them to death. And Saul said, There shall not a man be put to death this day; for today the Lord hath wrought salvation in Israel" (I Sam. 11:12,13). After Saul had been anointed king and the people had accepted him,

"Certain worthless fellows said, How shall this man save us? And they despised him, and brought him no presents. But he held his peace" (10:27).

At the beginning of his reign, Saul had a good relationship with the people who did not like him. But all leaders have their critics. All those in places of leadership and authority have people who won't follow them. These "worthless fellows" created problems for Saul, but he kept his mouth shut. Sometimes it's good for a leader to have a "deaf ear" and a "blind eye." Insurrection and rebellion must be dealt with sometimes, but in this case, it was wise to ignore the idle gossip and the criticism of these "worthless fellows."

After Saul had won this great victory, his respect increased in the nation. It's one thing to have *authority* and another to have *respect*. People give you authority, but you have to earn respect. When a man becomes the pastor of a church, the people give him authority when they install him; but he has to earn their respect. Saul had earned the respect of some people, and they said, "Let's get rid of those in the camp who don't want him to be king." Sometimes your friends can do more damage to you than your enemies can! And often you face greater testing *after* the victory than you do during the battle.

What did Saul do? He ignored their suggestion. He said, "There will not be any retaliation." Saul had a forgiving spirit. I wonder if Saul was thinking of Leviticus 19:18: "Thou shalt not avenge, nor bear any grudge against the childen of thy people, but thou shalt love thy neighbor as thyself: I am the

29

Lord." Those of us who are New Testament Christians have the admonition of Romans 12:17,18: "Recompense to no man evil for evil. Provide things honest in the sight of all men. If it be possible, as much as lieth in you, live peaceably with all men." Living peaceably if possible is not compromise—it's courtesy. It's recognizing the fact that people are different and that we can't always please everyone. How did Saul face the challenge of the advice of his friends? He gave God the glory. He said, "The Lord has wrought salvation in Israel; no one is going to die."

At this point, Saul looked like a really great man. When a man uses his victories for God's glory and not for personal gain, that is a sign of greatness. It is too bad Saul did not keep this attitude. Unfortunately, he became proud and envious, and he tried to destroy those who opposed him, including David.

The Admonition of the Word

Saul faced the attack of the enemy by faith. He overcame the advice of his friends. In I Samuel 11:14—12:25 we have a third challenge: *the admonition of the Word.* "Then said Samuel to the people, Come, and let us go to Gilgal, and renew the kingdom there. And all the people went to Gilgal; and there they made Saul king before the Lord in Gilgal, and there they sacrificed sacrifices of peace offerings before the Lord, and there Saul and all the men of Israel rejoiced greatly" (11:14,15). Actually, Saul had a threefold coronation. He was anointed privately by Samuel (10:1), and then he was anointed at Mizpeh when the tribes got together (vv. 17-25). Now, at Gilgal, they held the official coronation where they offered sacrifices to the Lord and where Samuel addressed the people.

The emphasis of Samuel's sermon in I Samuel 12 is *faithfulness.* In verses 1-5 he reminded them of his own faithfulness. He said, "I have been serving you all these years. Have I been faithful?" The people responded, "You have been faithful!"

In verses 6-11 he reminded them of God's faithfulness. Samuel reviewed the history of Israel—how God had delivered them from Egypt, how He had delivered them during the period of the judges and how He cared for His people.

Then Samuel called on the people to be faithful (vv. 12-25). God is faithful, and He expects that same quality from His people. "Now, therefore, behold the king whom ye have chosen, and whom ye have desired! And, behold, the Lord hath set a king over you. If ye will fear the Lord, and serve him, and obey his voice, and not rebel against the commandment of the Lord, then shall both ye, and also the king who reigneth over you, continue following the Lord your God. But if ye will not obey the voice of the Lord, but rebel against the commandment of the Lord, then shall the hand of the Lord be against you, as it was against your fathers" (vv. 13-15). Samuel reminded the people that they had some responsibilities to fulfill. Just because Saul had won a victory, it did not mean the end—it was only the beginning.

First, they must fear God (v. 14). He mentioned this again in verse 24. They must also serve God. "Serve him and obey his voice" (v. 14). "Serve him in truth with all your heart; for consider how great things he hath done for you" (v. 24). Samuel warned Saul and the people that they must not rebel against the commandment of God. If they rebelled, God's hand would be against them. "And turn ye not aside: for then should ye go after vain things [idols], which cannot profit nor deliver; for they are vain" (v. 21).

At this coronation, Saul apparently accepted the admonition of the Word of God. He heeded Samuel's call to fear the Lord, serve Him, obey His voice and not rebel against His commandments. While Saul's intentions were good in the beginning, he later disobeyed every one of the Lord's admonitions. Instead of fearing God, he started fearing the people and the enemy; instead of serving the Lord, he began serving his own interests.

The life of Saul is a reminder to us that good beginnings are no guarantee of successful endings. May the Lord help us to realize that we must constantly fear Him, serve Him, obey Him and surrender to His will if we are to successfully face the challenges of life.

Chapter 4

Saul's First Defeat
(I Sam. 13)

Thus far, King Saul's record has been one of obedience and victory. He defeated the Ammonites and firmly established himself as Israel's hero and first king. The nation went to Gilgal and had a wonderful public coronation. Samuel preached a great sermon exhorting Saul and the people to be faithful to God.

But one victory does not make a man a conqueror. In I Samuel 13 the Philistines came on the scene, and Saul had to deal with them. You cannot live on yesterday's victories. Unfortunately, at this point in Saul's performance, he starts to change. He begins that downward spiral that ultimately led to defeat, disgrace and death.

"And the Philistines gathered themselves together to fight with Israel, thirty thousand chariots, and six thousand horsemen, and people as the sand which is on the seashore in multitude; and they came up, and encamped in Michmash, eastward from Beth-aven. When the men of Israel saw that they were hedged in (for the people were distressed), then the people did hide themselves in caves, and in thickets, and among rocks, and in high places, and in pits.

And some of the Hebrews went over the Jordan to the land of Gad and Gilead. As for Saul, he was yet in Gilgal, and all the people followed him trembling.

"And he tarried seven days, according to the set time that Samuel had appointed; but Samuel came not to Gilgal, and the people were scattered from him. And Saul said, Bring here a burnt offering to me, and peace offerings. And he offered the burnt offering. And it came to pass that, as soon as he had ceased offering the burnt offering, behold, Samuel came; and Saul went out to meet him, that he might bless him. And Samuel said, What hast thou done? And Saul said, Because I saw that the people were scattered from me, and that thou camest not within the days appointed, and that the Philistines gathered themselves together at Michmash, therefore, said I, The Philistines will come down now upon me to Gilgal, and I have not made supplication unto the Lord; I forced myself therefore, and offered a burnt offering. And Samuel said to Saul, Thou hast done foolishly: thou hast not kept the commandment of the Lord thy God, which he commanded thee; for now would the Lord have established thy kingdom upon Israel forever. But now thy kingdom shall not continue. The Lord hath sought him a man after his own heart, and the Lord hath commanded him to be captain over his people, because thou hast not kept that which the Lord commanded thee" (vv. 5-14).

What Saul did that day may not seem especially serious to us. He became impatient and offered the sacrifice before Samuel arrived. But actually what he did was a serious offense in the eyes of God—so serious that it cost Saul the kingdom. That day, Saul took three giant steps away from God and started on his downward path to defeat. We can also take those same three steps and start down the road to failure. What are the three dangerous steps? Unbelief, impatience and dishonesty. Although, on the surface, Saul's sin may not seem too great, it was the beginning of failure because he disobeyed God.

Unbelief

The first step was *unbelief*. "Samuel said, What hast thou done? And Saul said, Because I saw" (I Sam. 13:11). Saul started to walk by sight and not by faith. Jonathan, Saul's son, was the one who trusted God. Jonathan smote the garrison of the Philistines in Geba, and the Philistines launched a counterattack against Israel (see vv. 3-5). It was Jonathan who stepped out by faith and who began the battle. When Saul heard about it, he blew the trumpet and said, "Let the Hebrews hear. And all Israel heard it said that Saul had smitten the garrison of the Philistines, and that Israel also was held in abomination with the Philistines" (vv. 3,4). The literal meaning is that they became "a stench" to the Philistines. In other words, Jonathan said, "Let's get something going here!" So he attacked the garrison and forced the Philistines to act.

When Saul started to walk by sight and not by faith, he began to get into trouble. The enemy was gathered together like the sand on the seashore. When Saul saw all of those chariots and horsemen,

35

he knew he was facing a large army. Not only that, but Saul's own soldiers were deserting him. His army was hedged in and distressed. The men were hiding themselves and crossing the river to get away. They were trembling and they were scattered. Wherever Saul looked, he saw defeat.

His army was deserting, and besides that, the men did not have adequate weapons (vv. 19-23). To add difficulty to dismay, Samuel did not appear at the appointed time. Samuel had said, "And thou shalt go down before me to Gilgal; and behold, I will come down unto thee, to offer burnt offerings, and to sacrifice sacrifices of peace offerings: seven days shalt thou tarry, till I come to thee, and show thee what thou shalt do" (10:8). Saul waited and waited, but Samuel did not appear. Saul got tired of waiting and sacrificed the offerings without Samuel.

Saul forgot what had happened at Gilgal. When he had been publicly crowned king, Samuel had said, "Fear the Lord!" "Don't fear the enemy—fear the Lord, serve Him and obey His voice!" (see 12:24). Saul forgot that Samuel had reminded the people of all the past victories God had given to the nation. He forgot that Samuel had prayed to God and that a miracle had taken place: It rained during the harvest season (see vv. 17,18).

In spite of the effectiveness of Samuel's prayer and the encouragement of Israel's history, Saul became afraid and unbelief gripped his heart. He started to walk by sight and not by faith.

Samuel had said to him, "Fear the Lord" (vv. 14,24). When you fear the Lord, you don't need to fear anyone else. Before long Saul began to fear the people, then Goliath and then David. In the final battle he was so frightened that he consulted a witch.

Impatience

Saul's first step toward defeat was unbelief. His second step was *impatience*. Saul could not wait a week for Samuel to arrive. Faith and patience go together. In Hebrews 6:12 we read: "That ye be not slothful, but followers of them who through faith and patience inherit the promises." Hebrews 10:36 says, "For ye have need of patience that, after ye have done the will of God, ye might receive the promise." Faith and patience go together. We read in Isaiah 28:16: "He that believeth shall not make haste." Impatience is a mark of immaturity. "Knowing this, that the testing of your faith worketh patience. But let patience have her perfect work, that ye may be perfect and entire, lacking nothing" (James 1:3,4).

We have no evidence that Saul was very mature when it came to spiritual things. You will remember that he did not even know who Samuel was. He had no idea what Samuel could do for him. Saul became impatient and therefore rushed ahead of the Lord and lost his crown as a result. James 1:12 says, "Blessed is the man that endureth temptation; for when he is tried, he shall receive the crown of life, which the Lord hath promised to them that love him." Instead of receiving a heavenly crown, Saul lost his earthly crown because he became impatient.

37

It is interesting to note in I Samuel 13, 14 and 15 how Saul changes. In chapter 13 he ran ahead of the Lord. In chapter 14 he hesitated and vacillated. In chapter 15 he lagged behind. He knew what he was supposed to do, but he did not do it. Saul was unstable. Do you know why? "A double-minded man is unstable in all his ways" (James 1:8). Saul was double minded. At the beginning of his reign, he was concerned only about doing God's will. He was humble and yielded to the Lord. But after he won his first victory, he became a little proud. Unbelief moved in, and then Saul found himself in trouble because of impatience.

In Psalm 32:9 we read: "Be ye not like the horse, or like the mule." Saul was like both. Like the horse, he rushed ahead (I Sam. 13). Like the mule, he lagged behind (ch. 15). Saul forgot what had happened at Gilgal at the time of his coronation. He had forgotten that Samuel had given him all the assurance he needed. Samuel had encouraged him to trust God, but Saul's unbelief led him to fear the enemy. Samuel had said, "Obey His voice." But Saul became impatient and ran ahead of the Lord.

Dishonesty

The third downward step that Saul took was *dishonesty*. Saul rushed ahead and offered the burnt offering—and then Samuel arrived! Samuel said, "What hast thou done?" (I Sam. 13:11). Samuel could tell that something was wrong. Immediately Saul began to give excuses. In I Samuel 13 he blamed Samuel. You will notice that in chapter 14 he blamed Jonathan, and in chapter 15 he blamed the people. But Saul never blamed himself! He was good at making excuses. Saul said, "Because I saw that the people were scattered from me, and that thou camest not within the days appointed, and that the Philistines gathered themselves together at Michmash, therefore, said I, The Philistines will come down now upon me to Gilgal, and I have not made supplication unto the Lord; I forced myself therefore, and offered a burnt offering" (13:11,12).

A person who is good at thinking of excuses is rarely good at anything else. If you have ever worked with someone who always had an excuse, you knew he was not going to do his work right. Samuel had told Saul, "Only fear the Lord, and serve him in truth with all your heart" (12:24). Saul was not serving God in truth. He was double minded, had a deceitful heart and was dishonest. He blamed Samuel when he really should have blamed himself.

It is a tragedy when a person starts moving away from the Lord because of unbelief, impatience and dishonesty. Samuel said to Saul, "Thou hast done foolishly" (13:13). It is foolish to fear the enemy instead of God. It is foolish to run ahead of the Lord and try to tell Him what to do. It certainly is foolish to be dishonest and to lie about your sins. "Thou has not kept the commandment of the Lord thy God, which he commanded thee. . . . But now thy kingdom shall not continue" (vv. 13,14). Saul lost the kingdom, and later he lost his crown and even his life.

Samuel announced that the Lord had found a man after His own heart. That man was David. He had the heart of a shepherd—a heart of integrity. Psalm 78:72 says this about David: "So he fed them according to the integrity of his heart, and guided them by the skillfulness of his hands." It takes both integrity and skill to be a leader. Saul had skillful hands, but he did not have integrity. The opposite of integrity is duplicity—a divided heart. "A double-minded man is unstable in all his ways" (James 1:8). David had a believing heart, while Saul failed because of unbelief. David was patient; he waited for years before he received the throne. But Saul was impatient and impulsive. David was honest. When he sinned, he honestly confessed, "I have sinned against the Lord" (II Sam. 12:13). Saul did not admit his sin; he was deceitful. As far as Saul was concerned, it was always someone else's fault!

We don't have to commit a serious sin to start on that steep road that leads to disgrace, discipline and possibly death. Unbelief, impatience and dishonesty started Saul on the road to defeat. Let's take to heart the admonition of Samuel: "Fear God, obey His voice, serve Him in truth" (see I Sam. 12:14,24).

Chapter 5

Saul's Second Defeat
(I Sam. 14)

King Saul's first defeat came because he ran ahead of the Lord. His second defeat came because he hesitated and failed to act promptly when the Lord was ready to give a great victory. As you read I Samuel 14 you find that Jonathan is the real hero, not Saul; and yet at the end, Saul would have had his own son killed! When a believer is not following the Lord, he treats his friends like enemies and his enemies like friends. That is what Saul did. God gave a great victory that day, but King Saul was not really a part of the victory. Why? Because he was out of fellowship with God. Let's consider the four stages in this battle and see how King Saul responded in each stage. We will see what happens when a person's fellowship with the Lord is broken.

You and I are in a battle. The Christian life is not a playground, it's a battleground. We are not wrestling against flesh and blood but against Satan and all of his hosts (see Eph. 6:12). We have many enemies—the world, the flesh, the Devil and those who oppose the things of the Lord. We know that Jesus Christ has already won the victory at Calvary. You and I are not fighting *for* victory; we are fighting *from* victory. The war has been won, but we still must fight the battles of which we all are a part. Where are you in relation to the battle?

Let me give you a simple outline of I Samuel 14, which describes the four stages of Saul's experience. In the battle with the Philistines, Jonathan won a great victory for the Lord, but Saul was on the fringes. In verses 1-15 Saul is *ignorant of the battle.* In verses 16-23 Saul is *watching* the battle. In verses 24-45 he is *hindering* the battle; and in verse 46 we find him *retreating* from the battle.

In verses 47-52 we have a summary of the victories that Saul won in subsequent years. Keep in mind that these victories were possible because of what Jonathan had done that day. He actually led the nation to victory.

Ignorant of the Battle

In the first stage Saul is *ignorant of the battle* (I Sam. 14:1-15). Jonathan said to his armor-bearer, "Come, and let us go over to the Philistines' garrison, that is on the other side. But he told not his father" (v. 1). I wonder if Jonathan realized that his father was not in fellowship with the Lord? If so, why bother to tell him about what he was going to do? While Jonathan was fighting the battle, Saul was doing nothing. We read in verse 2: "And Saul tarried in the farthest part of Gibeah under a pomegranate tree which is in Migron: and the people who were with him were about six hundred men." It's interesting that with an enemy to fight and a battle to win,

Saul and his 600 men were tarrying. Saul did not seek the Lord's will concerning the battle. Jonathan, on the other hand, was trusting God for a great victory. "It may be that the Lord will work for us; for there is no restraint to the Lord to save by many or by few" (v. 6).

What Jonathan did that day was, first of all, a great act of courage. He and his armor-bearer faced a huge army, and the two men showed tremendous courage. It was also an act of great faith. Jonathan trusted the Lord to win the battle. The Lord is not limited by numbers. Jonathan must have remembered what Gideon had learned about testing God's guidance and trusting God's power. "So the Lord saved Israel that day; and the battle passed over unto Beth-aven" (v. 23). Their attack was also an act of unselfishness. Jonathan could not inherit the kingdom. God had made it very clear to Saul, when he had run ahead of the Lord, that no one in his family would inherit the crown. And yet Jonathan still fought Israel's battles even though he could never be king.

Saul was ignorant of the fact that a battle was going on! The Philistines fell before Jonathan and his armor-bearer, and there was a great slaughter. "And there was trembling in the host, in the field, ... and the earth quaked" (v. 15).

It is amazing what one or two people can do if they just trust the Lord. Your church may not be winning many battles, and you may be discouraged. You don't have to call a big committee meeting or get the whole congregation together in order to have victory. Just find a Jonathan and an armor-bearer. Trust God and start doing His will, and He will give you great victories. One person can accomplish great deeds when he puts his trust in the Lord.

Watching the Battle

In stage two Saul is *watching the battle* (I Sam. 14:16-23). Saul's lookouts were watching the Philistine army, and they saw the enemy soldiers falling! The watchmen told Saul that the Philistines were dying, and Saul wondered why. Then he discovered that Jonathan and his armor-bearer were missing, so Saul asked the priest to bring the ark of God. Perhaps he wanted to carry the ark into the battle, or maybe he wanted to inquire about the will of the Lord. But then Saul changed his mind and decided to enter the battle.

One minute Saul was watching the battle, then he was inquiring of the Lord, and then he was deciding to fight. Why would Saul inquire of the Lord when a victory was in progress? Why would he pause to see what God wanted him to do when he could see the enemy retreating (v. 16); his own soldiers, who had defected, revolting against the Philistines (v. 21) and the soldiers, who had fled, returning (v. 22)? In the midst of all this, what was Saul doing? He was hesitating. "A double-minded man is unstable in all his ways" (James 1:8).

Someone has said that there are three kinds of people in our churches today: those who make things happen, those who watch things happen and

44

those who don't know that anything is happening! Jonathan and his armor-bearer were making things happen because they had faith in God. Saul was watching things happen; he was a useless spectator. Are you a spectator in the great battle of life? Are you allowing others to fight the battle for you?

Hindering the Battle

Before long, the situation grew worse. Soon Saul was *hindering the battle* (I Sam. 14:24-45). He hindered the battle in three different ways. First, his motive was wrong. "And the men of Israel were distressed that day; for Saul had solemnly charged the people, saying, Cursed be the man who eateth any food until evening, that I may be avenged on mine enemies" (v. 24). He was motivated by vengeance and pride, not by the glory of God. When Jonathan talked about the battle, the Lord was magnified. "The Lord will work for us; for there is no restraint to the Lord to save by many or by few" (v. 6). Jonathan continually gave the Lord the glory, but Saul tried to glorify himself. He said that he would punish his enemies. His motive was wrong, and that hindered the battle.

Second, he made a very foolish vow. He said, "Anyone who eats before evening will be cursed" (see v. 24). The army had to agree with this, and consequently, they became very hungry and could not fight very well.

I think that Saul made this vow just to appear very "spiritual." While Jonathan was out fighting the battle, Saul had to look like a spiritual leader. What

45

did he do? He called for the ark, and he asked the priest to determine the will of God but then interrupted him (v. 19). He then put the solemn vow on the army (v. 24). All of this looked very religious, but it actually weakened the army. We read that they were faint and distressed, or fatigued (vv. 24,28). Verse 31 says that the people were *very* faint. You can't fight a battle without nourishment.

Worse than that, when evening finally came, the soldiers rushed greedily upon the spoil, killed the sheep and oxen and started to eat the meat with the blood still in it (v. 32). By his foolish vow Saul had weakened the army and then led the people into sin. Jews were never supposed to eat meat with blood in it. Saul found a large stone and said, "Bring all of your food here and sacrifice it on this rock so the blood can drain out" (see vv. 33,34). He started to build an altar (v. 35), but he never quite finished it. The Hebrew reads: "With this stone he began to build." That was Saul's great problem: He would start things and never finish them.

He hindered the battle by his selfish motive, by a foolish vow and then by a very rash oath. He inquired of the Lord, but the Lord did not answer. Saul said that whoever was to blame would die, and Jonathan was singled out. What had Jonathan done? He had eaten some food (see vv. 36-43). Jonathan had not heard the oath; therefore, he was not obligated to obey it. He had not assented to the oath and knew nothing about it until the people told him (see vv. 27,28). Notice what Jonathan said in verse 29: "My father hath troubled the land; see, I pray you, how mine eyes have become bright, because I tasted a little of this honey." In other words, if they had eaten some of the honey that Jonathan found, they would have been much stronger and would have been able to have a greater victory.

Jonathan was taken aside, and Saul announced that his son would have to die (see v. 44). This is foolish, isn't it? Once again, I think Saul was trying to appear very spiritual. It was as if he said, "I have made an oath, and I will keep my oath." Saul blamed Samuel in chapter 13, and now he blamed Jonathan! In Saul's eyes it was always someone else's fault.

First, Saul was ignorant of the battle because he had not asked the Lord what to do. He didn't know that Jonathan was trusting the Lord for a victory. Then he was watching the battle because he was double minded and couldn't decide what to do, even though he could see that victory was assured. Then he was hindering the battle by his selfish motive, his foolish vow and his rash oath.

Retreating From the Battle

In I Samuel 14:46 we find him *retreating from the battle.* Instead of having the army rush ahead and win the victory, Saul led them in a retreat. Verse 46 says, "Then Saul went up from following the Philistines; and the Philistines went to their own place." If the army had eaten properly and had followed Jonathan's leadership, they could have swooped down on the Philistine army and won a great victory. But instead, they were delaying and hesitating. Saul blamed everyone but himself. This is what happens to spiritual leaders when they turn away from the Lord. Often, great things are happening, but they know nothing about them.

What a contrast is seen between Jonathan and Saul! Jonathan was a man of action, but Saul was a man of empty words and broken promises. Jonathan showed great faith, while Saul tried to appear religious with his vows and his oaths. Jonathan was bold and courageous, while Saul hesitated and waited. Jonathan was wise, but Saul said and did foolish things. Jonathan brought out the best in the army, while Saul brought out the worst in it!

Are you experiencing defeat or victory in your life? "And this is the victory that overcometh the world, even our faith" (I John 5:4). Let's not be like Saul but like Jonathan. Let's trust God to work for us and enter the battle claiming His victory.

Chapter 6

Saul's Third Defeat
(I Sam. 15)

If any man had a reason to become a success, it was Saul, the first king of Israel. In the beginning, everything was in his favor. He had a divine call from God, and he had the power of God's Spirit to enable him to do what God wanted. He had a wonderful praying friend in Samuel the prophet, and he had a group of men who supported him. Yet God had to discipline Saul because of his disobedience and lack of trust. Saul went down in history as a great failure at a time when the nation of Israel needed a great success. He lost God's blessing, his crown and his life.

How do you explain a tragedy such as this? Well, Saul was to blame for his own failure. He abandoned God's way and began to live on substitutes.

I Samuel 15 tells us how Saul began to live on substitutes: "Samuel also said unto Saul, The Lord sent me to anoint thee as king over his people, over Israel; now, therefore, hearken thou to the voice of the words of the Lord. Thus saith the Lord of hosts, I remember that which Amalek did to Israel, how he laid wait for him in the way, when he [Israel] came

49

up from Egypt. Now go and smite Amalek, and utterly destroy all that they have, and spare them not" (vv. 1-3).

The Lord gave Saul a divine commission; He was actually giving Saul another chance to prove his faith. In chapter 13 Saul was like a horse because he ran ahead of the Lord, but in chapter 15 he was like a mule. He did not fully obey the Lord.

I Samuel 15:7 tells us that Saul smote the Amalekites. But "he took Agag, the king of the Amalekites, alive, and utterly destroyed all the people with the edge of the sword. But Saul and the people spared Agag, and the best of the sheep, and of the oxen, and of the fatlings, and the lambs, and all that was good, and would not utterly destroy them; but everything that was vile and refuse, that they destroyed utterly. Then came the word of the Lord unto Samuel, saying, It repenteth me that I have set up Saul to be king; for he is turned back from following me, and hath not performed my commandments. And it grieved Samuel, and he cried unto the Lord all night" (vv. 8-11).

How many friends do you have who would pray all night for you? Samuel wrestled with God all night because of the disobedience of King Saul. "And when Samuel rose early to meet Saul in the morning, it was told Samuel, saying, Saul came to Carmel, and, behold, he set him up a place [literally, a monument], and is gone about, and passed on, and gone down to Gilgal" (v. 12). Perhaps Saul was trying to avoid Samuel.

"And Samuel came to Saul. And Saul said unto

him, Blessed be thou of the Lord; I have performed the commandment of the Lord. And Samuel said, What meaneth, then, this bleating of the sheep in mine ears, and the lowing of the oxen which I hear? And Saul said, They [the people] have brought them from the Amalekites; for the people spared the best of the sheep and of the oxen, to sacrifice unto the Lord thy God; and the rest we have utterly destroyed" (vv. 13-15).

Saying Rather Than Doing

As you read this account, you can see how Saul was living on substitutes. To begin with, *he substituted saying for doing.* "Saul said unto him, Blessed be thou of the Lord; I have performed the commandment of the Lord" (I Sam. 15:13). But he had *not* performed the commandment of the Lord! What was God's commandment? Utterly destroy the Amalekites.

The Amalekites were old enemies of the Jews. "Then came Amalek, and fought with Israel in Rephidim. And Moses said unto Joshua, Choose us out men, and go out, fight with Amalek: tomorrow I will stand on the top of the hill with the rod of God in mine hand" (Ex. 17:8,9). Moses stood on top of the mountain praying while Joshua was in the valley fighting. With the Lord's help, Moses and Joshua defeated Amalek and his people.

Exodus 17:14 is a key verse: "And the Lord said unto Moses, Write this for a memorial in a book, and rehearse it in the ears of Joshua; for I will utterly put out the remembrance of Amalek from under

51

heaven." That was God's decree that the Amalekites were not going to survive.

Deuteronomy 25 contains a similar statement
where Moses is addressing Joshua and the people
before they go into the Promised Land: "Remember
what Amalek did unto thee by the way, when ye
were come forth out of Egypt; how he met thee by
the way, and smote those behind thee, even all that
were feeble behind thee, when thou wast faint and
weary; and he feared not God. Therefore it shall be,
when the Lord thy God hath given thee rest from all
thine enemies round about, in the land which the
Lord thy God giveth thee for an inheritance, to
possess it, that thou shalt blot out the remembrance of Amalek from under heaven; thou shalt
not forget it" (vv. 17-19).

Moses was required to record these words in
Deuteronomy and to make sure the people remembered God's pronouncement upon Amalek. So
from both Exodus and Deuteronomy, Saul should
have known that Amalek was to be completely
destroyed. The Prophet Samuel had also told Saul
of God's commandment to completely destroy
Amalek, and yet Saul spared the king and the best
of the spoil.

Then Saul told a lie. He claimed to be obedient
when he was really disobedient. God knew that
Saul was lying, as did Samuel; before long, even the
people knew about Saul's lie. The bleating of the
sheep and the lowing of the oxen were clear evidence that he had not obeyed God. Saul was substituting saying for doing.

It's so easy for us as God's people to substitute words for actions. But God does not want words in place of actions. We are not to be only hearers of the Word; we are to be *doers* of the Word (see James 1:22).

Three times in I John 1 the Apostle John referred to saying one thing but doing another. "If we say that we have fellowship with him, and walk in darkness, we lie, and do not the truth" (v. 6). "If we say that we have no sin, we deceive ourselves, and the truth is not in us" (v. 8). "If we say that we have not sinned, we make him a liar, and his word is not in us" (v. 10). In verse 6 we are lying to *others;* in verse 8 we are lying to *ourselves;* and in verse 10 we are trying to lie to *God.*

This results in a terrible deterioration of character through disobedience and deceit. How easy it is for us to sing songs, quote verses and say prayers without ever allowing the words to affect our lives. Our spiritual life becomes nothing but words. Beware when you start substituting saying for doing.

Excuses Rather Than Confession

A second substitution took place that day. Saul *substituted excuses for confession.* In I Samuel 15:15 Saul tried to excuse his disobedience by claiming that the animals were only kept to be sacrificed to God: "And Saul said, They have brought them from the Amalekites; for the people spared the best of the sheep and of the oxen, to sacrifice

53

unto the Lord thy God; and the rest we have utterly destroyed." Saul then tried to excuse his behavior by putting the blame on the people in verse 21: "But the people took of the spoil, sheep and oxen, the chief of the things which should have been utterly destroyed, to sacrifice unto the Lord thy God in Gilgal." King Saul was very good at excuses. Beware of excuses! Billy Sunday used to define an excuse as "the skin of a reason stuffed with a lie."

In chapter 13 Saul's excuse was that he blamed Samuel. Samuel did not arrive when he had said he would, so Saul went ahead and offered the sacrifice. In chapter 14 Saul blamed Jonathan for the defeat of Israel because he had eaten a small portion of honey when the army was under a vow. Here in chapter 15 Saul blamed the people when he failed to obey God's command to destroy the Amalekites.

Watch out for people who always have an excuse. An excuse is a refusal to be honest and to accept responsibility for our actions. Saul should have confessed his sin honestly. "He that covereth his sins shall not prosper, but whoso confesseth and forsaketh them shall have mercy" (Prov. 28:13). One sin often leads to another when we try to hide our sin.

When Saul began his career as king, he was humble, obedient and responsible. He had the respect of the people and the blessing of God. But the more he was elevated, the greater his moral decline became, until finally the Lord said, "It repenteth me that I have set up Saul to be king; for he is turned back from following me" (I Sam. 15:11).

54

What decay took place in Saul's life because he substituted excuses for confession!

If you and I have disobeyed God, we must be honest about it and confess our sin. "If we confess our sins, he is faithful and just to forgive us our sins, and to cleanse us from all unrighteousness" (I John 1:9).

Sacrifice Rather Than Obedience

Finally, Saul *substituted sacrifice for obedience.* He said, "I have obeyed the word of the Lord. We have taken this spoil that we might be able to sacrifice it to the Lord" (see I Sam. 15:15). And yet we know that God does not want sacrifice—He wants obedience. As Samuel said in verse 22, "Hath the Lord as great delight in burnt offerings and sacrifices, as in obeying the voice of the Lord? Behold, to obey is better than sacrifice, and to hearken than the fat of rams."

Many verses in Scripture confirm this. Psalm 50:12-14 says, "If I were hungry, I would not tell thee; for the world is mine, and all the fullness thereof. Will I eat the flesh of bulls, or drink the blood of goats? Offer unto God thanksgiving, and pay thy vows unto the Most High." God does not need our sacrifices; He would rather have our worship. David said in Psalm 51:16,17, "For thou desirest not sacrifice, else would I give it; thou delightest not in burnt offering. The sacrifices of God are a broken spirit; a broken and a contrite heart, O God, thou wilt not despise." Saul did not have a broken spirit. I Samuel 15:23 says, "For rebellion is as the

55

sin of witchcraft, and stubbornness is as iniquity and idolatry."

We read in Isaiah 1:11: "To what purpose is the multitude of your sacrifices unto me? saith the Lord." Hosea 6:6 says, "For I desired mercy, and not sacrifice, and the knowledge of God more than burnt offerings." In Micah 6:7,8 we are told, "Will the Lord be pleased with thousands of rams, or with ten thousands of rivers of oil? . . . He hath shown thee, O man, what is good; and what doth the Lord require of thee, but to do justly, and to love mercy, and to walk humbly with thy God?"

Throughout Scripture God makes it very clear that He wants obedience rather than sacrifice. Sacrifice can never replace surrender. Psalm 119:162 says, "I rejoice at thy word, as one that findeth great spoil." The psalmist wanted the Word of God more than great spoil, but Saul wanted great spoil more than he wanted to obey the Word of God.

Saul substituted saying for doing. He substituted excuses for confession. He substituted sacrifice for obedience. No wonder he failed!

We must be careful not to substitute empty words or outward displays of spirituality for true service and obedience to God. Obedience leads to victory, while disobedience leads to defeat. When we do disobey the Lord, we need to be honest about it. We must confess our sins; when we do, God in His mercy forgives us. Don't try to hide your sin by making excuses as Saul did. It only leads to heartache and failure. We can't know success if we try to live on substitutes.

56

Chapter 7

Saul's Third Defeat (cont.)
(I Sam. 15)

When you consider the sin of King Saul, as recorded in I Samuel 15, you realize how terrible it is to rebel against God. King Saul began to live on substitutes. He substituted saying for doing. He said, "I have performed the commandment of the Lord" (v. 13). Then he substituted excuses for confession. "But the people took of the spoil, sheep and oxen, the chief of the things which should have been utterly destroyed, to sacrifice unto the Lord thy God in Gilgal" (v. 21). It's tragic when a person tries to live on excuses. In chapter 13 Saul blamed Samuel for not showing up earlier. In chapter 14 he blamed Jonathan for eating when the army was under a vow. In chapter 15 he blamed the people.

Saul also substituted sacrifice for obedience. He said, "We have spared all these things to sacrifice them to the Lord" (see v. 15). How can we sacrifice to the Lord what God has condemned? The people thought it was the best, the chief of all the spoil, but God looked at all that livestock and said, "I don't want it. I want the obedience of your heart. I want your will to be yielded to Me."

It's so easy for us to want to sacrifice something—time, money, work at the church. We think that this compensates for our disobedience, but it cannot. God wants absolute surrender and obedience from us. Samuel asked, "Hath the Lord as great delight in burnt offerings and sacrifices, as in obeying the voice of the Lord? Behold, to obey is better than sacrifice, and to hearken than the fat of rams" (v. 22).

Reputation Rather Than Character

Saul made a fourth substitution: He *substituted reputation for character.* "And Saul said unto Samuel, I have sinned; for I have transgressed the commandment of the Lord, and thy words, because I feared the people, and obeyed their voice. Now, therefore, I pray thee, pardon my sin, and turn again with me, that I may worship the Lord. And Samuel said unto Saul, I will not return with thee; for thou hast rejected the word of the Lord, and the Lord hath rejected thee from being king over Israel. And as Samuel turned about to go away, he laid hold upon the skirt of his mantle, and it tore. And Samuel said unto him, The Lord hath torn the kingdom of Israel from thee this day, and hath given it to a neighbor of thine, who is better than thou. And also the Strength of Israel will not lie nor repent; for he is not a man, that he should repent. Then he said, I have sinned; yet honor me now, I pray thee, before the elders of my people, and before Israel, and turn again with me, that I may worship the Lord thy God.

So Samuel turned again after Saul; and Saul worshiped the Lord" (I Sam. 15:24-31). Saul was only concerned about his reputation with the people. He was not concerned about his character or what God thought of him.

Twice in this passage he said, "I have sinned" (vv. 24,30). I wonder how sincere this confession really was. A number of people in the Bible made this same confession, "I have sinned." Pharaoh said it to Moses (see Ex. 9:27;10:16), but he certainly didn't mean it. Balaam used these same words, "I have sinned" (Num. 22:34); and yet Balaam turned out to be a reprobate prophet. Achan said it (see Josh. 7:20). David said it, but when he said it, he really meant it: "I have sinned against the Lord" (II Sam. 12:13).

Saul twice said, "I have sinned," but I don't think he really meant it. He was concerned only about his reputation and not about his character. Abraham Lincoln once said that reputation and character may be compared to a tree. Character is the tree, and reputation is the shadow that is cast by the tree. Reputation is what men think we are; character is what God knows we are. D. L. Moody once said that character is what a person is in the dark, when no one is watching.

Throughout his official career, Saul's great concern was "What do people think of me?" He stood head and shoulders above everyone else; he was good looking, strong and courageous. But he did not possess a godly character. You never find Saul doing the things David did—singing praises to God

59

or serving Him with integrity of heart. Saul substituted reputation for character.

If you start living to please people, you are going to be in trouble. You may be in Christian service and say, "Well, a lot of people are watching me." Do what *God* wants you to do, and don't live to please people. If you start thinking only of your reputation, you will start doing what Saul did—cutting corners and making excuses. You will be caught between God and people. Don't fear people. "The fear of man bringeth a snare," says Proverbs 29:25. Don't worry about receiving the honor or praise of people. The important thing is personal integrity. God never called us to be popular or to have a great reputation. He called us to be honest and faithful. He wants to build our character.

His Will Rather Than God's Will

Saul substituted saying for doing, excuses for confession, sacrifice for obedience and reputation for character. Finally, he *substituted his will for God's will*. You and I may look at Saul's sin and say, "He spared Agag, the king, and some of the spoil. That can't be too bad." But it was sin. First Samuel 15:23 says, "For rebellion is as the sin of witchcraft, and stubbornness is as iniquity and idolatry. Because thou hast rejected the word of the Lord, he hath also rejected thee from being king" (see also v. 26).

God had warned Saul about rebellion. When the kingship was confirmed at Gilgal, the warning was given: "But if ye will not obey the voice of the Lord, but rebel against the commandment of the Lord, then shall the hand of the Lord be against you, as it was against your fathers" (12:15). We read in I Samuel 12:24: "Only fear the Lord, and serve him in truth with all your heart." When you fear the Lord, you don't have to fear the enemy; but in chapter 14 Saul was afraid of the enemy. You don't have to be afraid of people, but in chapter 15 Saul was afraid of the people. In chapter 17 Saul was afraid of Goliath, but David wasn't because he trusted the Lord. In chapter 18 you will find Saul was afraid of David; and in chapter 28 Saul was afraid of the great enemy army that was about to attack.

When you fear the Lord, you don't have to be afraid of anything else. The person of integrity is concerned only with serving God and doing His will.

Saul substituted his will for God's will, and this was the sin of rebellion. No wonder God rejected him! When you stop to consider the matter, you realize that Saul was the loser: He lost his character, and he lost his crown. God rejected him from being king. Instead of winning a great victory that would have glorified God, Saul lost the battle and went down in shameful defeat. He lost his good friend, Samuel. "And Samuel came no more to see Saul until the day of his death; nevertheless, Samuel mourned for Saul" (15:35).

Saul lost God's blessing. God would have given great blessing to Saul, but he couldn't because Saul had not proved himself trustworthy. Saul lost God's Spirit. "But the Spirit of the Lord departed from Saul, and an evil spirit from the Lord troubled him"

61

(16:14). If you are going to rebel against God, then you will have to suffer the consequences. This helps us understand why David prayed after he had sinned, "Take not thy holy Spirit from me" (Ps. 51:11). He saw what had happened to King Saul, and he did not want it to happen in his own life. Finally, King Saul lost his life. Because he disobeyed God, he ended up committing suicide on the battlefield when he could have won a great victory for the Lord.

May this be a warning to us not to live on substitutes! Don't submit to your own desires instead of obeying God's will. God uses the person who seeks to glorify Him, while self-glorification only leads to defeat.

Thinking of Saul reminds us of another Saul in the Bible, Saul of Tarsus. He was also from the tribe of Benjamin. King Saul stood head and shoulders above everyone else when he was anointed, and yet he was humble in the beginning. When he was little in his own eyes, God could bless him; but then he became proud and disobeyed God. Saul of Tarsus was a great man in terms of *stature*. He was a leading religious leader in his day. But when he became a Christian, he realized how small he was. He changed his name to Paul, which means "little." Saul of Tarsus was greatly used by God. He called himself "the chief of sinners" (see I Tim. 1:15). He made no excuses. Instead, he obeyed God and made sacrifices for Him. He put character before reputation. He was criticized, abused and lied about, but still he obeyed God.

When we contrast Saul of Tarsus and King Saul, we realize how grievous it is to sin and how blessed it is to live for the Lord. Saul of Tarsus was a man of integrity and character who obeyed God. His great desire was to fulfill his course and to accomplish the work God had called him to do. He wasn't concerned about his reputation, even though people lied about him and accused him. Whenever he sinned, he confessed it to the Lord. Because he practiced what he preached, no one could look at his life and accuse him of being a hypocrite. He wanted to do the will of God above all else; as a result, Saul of Tarsus (who became Paul the apostle) won his crown. "Henceforth there is laid up for me a crown of righteousness, which the Lord, the righteous judge, shall give me at that day; and not to me only, but unto all them also that love his appearing" (II Tim. 4:8). King Saul lost the power of the Holy Spirit, but Saul of Tarsus was filled mightily with the Holy Spirit of God.

It's wonderful to win your crown, to have praying friends who believe in you and to enjoy the blessing of God. When you are trusting the Lord, you aren't worried about being honored before people. You don't have to find some new excuse to cover up a sin you have committed.

We need to be little in our own eyes—to realize that we are nothing apart from the Lord. We should be able to say as John the Baptist did, "He must increase, but I must decrease" (John 3:30).

Your character is a priceless possession. Don't ruin it. Your opportunities to serve the Lord are invaluable. Don't waste them. The abilities that God has given you are His gifts to be used for His glory. Don't abuse them.

No one had a greater opportunity to succeed than King Saul did. Everything was in his favor. He could have gone from victory to victory, but instead he failed because he did not have integrity. Therefore, God rejected him and chose David, who had the right heart: "The Lord hath sought him a man after his own heart" (I Sam. 13:14).

Only the Lord can help us build Christian character. May the Lord help us to walk in His will. Yield to His will and bring glory to His name by doing what He has called you to do.

Chapter 8

Fighting the Wrong Enemy
(I Sam. 16-23)

Has anyone in your life ever really broken your heart because he or she rebelled against the Lord? You did your best for them, prayed for them and encouraged them, but they failed you and the Lord. It hurts down inside, doesn't it?

If you have had that experience, then you know how Samuel felt when King Saul rebelled against the Lord and disobeyed His Word. "Then Samuel went to Ramah; and Saul went up to his house to Gibeah of Saul. And Samuel came no more to see Saul until the day of his death; nevertheless, Samuel mourned for Saul. And the Lord repented that he had made Saul king over Israel" (I Sam. 15:34,35).

When it says that God repented, it does not mean that God made a mistake. He knows everything, including future events; but the writer used human language here to express divine truth. God responds to our failures. He is hurt when we fail. Just as a child hurts his father when he rebels against him, so God's heart was broken when Saul rebelled against Him.

But disobedient men cannot hinder God's plan or

stop Him from working. Even if we are not faithful, God is faithful and will accomplish His purposes. But we will miss the blessing of seeing God work through us. God knows what He is doing, and He always has someone ready to step in and do the job and share the blessing. In this case it was David.

I Samuel 16:1 says, "And the Lord said unto Samuel, How long wilt thou mourn for Saul, seeing I have rejected him from reigning over Israel?" The Hebrew word translated "mourn" means to grieve for the dead. Samuel mourned for Saul as though he were dead. Perhaps he was praying that Saul would repent and that God might change His mind. But God had other plans. "Fill thine horn with oil, and go; I will send thee to Jesse, the Bethlehemite; for I have provided me a king among his sons" (v. 1).

David was taking care of the sheep when Samuel arrived with his horn of anointing oil, so his family had to call him in from the fields (see vv. 4-12). Samuel anointed David, and "the Spirit of the Lord came upon David from that day onward" (v. 13). David was anointed, while Saul was abandoned. "But the Spirit of the Lord departed from Saul, and an evil spirit from the Lord troubled him" (v. 14). Saul did not want to follow God; therefore, God could not entrust the Holy Spirit's power to him.

In verses 15-23 Saul and David are brought together by God. God brought David into Saul's life because Saul needed David's help. "An evil spirit from the Lord troubled him [Saul]" (v. 14). Saul was being disciplined by God because of his disobedience. The only way he could find relief was to have someone play music that would bring peace to his heart. When Saul wanted a musician, one of his servants told him, "Behold, I have seen a son of Jesse, the Bethlehemite, who is skillful in playing, and a mighty, valiant man, and a man of war, and prudent in matters, and an agreeable person, and the Lord is with him" (v. 18). Those are some credentials, aren't they?

Saul sent for David and brought him into his court; this was the beginning of a stirring drama involving David and Saul, a drama in which the forces of evil attack the forces of God. But this drama is not ancient history; it continues today in homes, in churches and in communities. Wherever you find someone who is being blessed of God in contact with someone who has been abandoned by God, you find conflict. This drama continues from chapter 16 to chapter 31 of I Samuel, and it falls into three acts: Act I, Saul loved David (chs. 16,17); Act II, Saul envied David (chs. 18-20); and Act III, Saul exiled David and tried to kill him (chs. 21-31).

Saul Loved David

The first act in the drama is recorded in chapters 16 and 17: *Saul loved David.* First Samuel 16:21 sounds peculiar when you know the end of the story: "And David came to Saul, and stood before him; and he loved him greatly; and he became his armor-bearer." It's interesting to note that a loving relationship existed in the beginning between Saul and David. Saul gave David two particular tasks. First of all, David was his armor-bearer. That was an

67

important title to have and an honorable place to serve, for he helped Saul in his battles. He was also the court musician. Whenever Saul experienced one of his attacks, David would sing and play his harp, and this would calm him down. "And Saul sent to Jesse, saying, Let David, I pray thee, stand before me; for he hath found favor in my sight" (v. 22).

This was a temporary position for David in the beginning. In I Samuel 17:15 we read: "But David went and returned from Saul to feed his father's sheep at Bethlehem." The Hebrew reads: "But David went back and forth between home and Saul." But after David killed Goliath, he was given a permanent position in Saul's court. "And Saul took him that day, and would let him go no more home to his father's house" (18:2). So what began as a temporary position became a permanent position when David was placed in charge of the king's bodyguard (see v. 5).

In the beginning Saul loved David, but "can two walk together, except they be agreed?" (Amos 3:3). What fellowship does light have with darkness? (see II Cor. 6:14). What fellowship can the Spirit have with the flesh? Saul lived for himself, while David lived for others. Saul was proud and rebellious, while David was humble and obedient.

Saul Envied David

This leads us to I Samuel 18-20, the second act in this drama: *Saul envied David.* David "behaved himself wisely" (18:5,14,15). He walked according

68

to the will of the Lord, he battled victoriously, and he won the admiration of the people; but he was not ruined by their praise. Women came out when he returned from battle, dancing and singing. They chanted, "Saul hath slain his thousands, and David his ten thousands. And Saul was very angry, and the saying displeased him" (vv. 7,8). David responded to this praise with humility, but Saul responded with fear, anger and envy.

Proverbs 27:21 says, "As the refining pot for silver, and the furnace for gold, so is a man to his praise." Just as the heat of the refining pot or the furnace separates the impurities from the silver or the gold, so also praise will reveal what is in a person, bringing out either his best or his worst.

The praise given to David brought out the best in him and revealed his humility. But the praise that David received brought out the worst in Saul. Saul became envious of David. The next day, the evil spirit came upon Saul as David played, and Saul picked up his javelin and tried to kill David.

Then Saul removed David from his position as court musician and captain of the bodyguard and made him captain over a thousand men and sent him out into battle. He was hoping that the Philistines would kill David.

Saul had promised to give David his eldest daughter, Merab, for his wife. But he deceived David and gave her to someone else. Then David asked for Michal to be his wife. Saul was plotting against David the entire time. For a dowry Saul required David to kill 100 Philistines and bring back their

69

foreskins. He was hoping that David would be killed in the process. But, instead, David killed 200 of the enemy in order to win his wife! (see I Sam. 18:17-27). "And Saul was yet the more afraid of David; and Saul became David's enemy continually" (v. 29).

First, Saul loved David; then he envied David and tried to kill him. Saul even told his son Jonathan to kill him (19:1). Saul also sent men to David's house to bring him back so Saul could kill him, but Michal deceived Saul, and David escaped (vv. 11-18). Then Saul went down to Ramah, intending to kill David, but again he failed (vv. 19-24).

It is remarkable that the man who began by loving David was now envying David and trying to destroy him. That's what envy does to you. Envy is like a cancer of the soul that eats away at you. When you allow yourself to become jealous of another's possessions or accomplishments, envy grows until it takes complete control of your life and begins to destroy you. David was being used by God, and the people saw that he was a man of true spiritual stature. He had earned the respect and admiration of the people and therefore had become a threat to Saul's position. Saul became so envious of David's popularity with the people that killing David became an obsession with him. Saul allowed envy to control him, and it began to destroy him.

Saul Exiled David

This leads us to the third act in this drama: *Saul exiled David.* In I Samuel 21-31 David is on the run. He was continually forced to flee from Saul. He went to Ahimelech, the priest, and then to Achish, king of Gath, and then to the cave of Adullam. During all of these years, David was a fugitive in the wilderness of Judah. If you have ever seen the wilderness of Judah, you know how dry and dangerous and difficult a place it is.

All of this brought out the worst in Saul. He became obsessed with chasing David and destroying him. It was a foolish thing to attempt because David was God's anointed, and God was watching over him.

But all of these trials brought out the *best* in David. He wrote 20 wonderful psalms during this period of exile. Looking at a few verses from these psalms will help us to see David's attitude while he was in exile. Psalm 34:1,6 says, "I will bless the Lord at all times; his praise shall continually be in my mouth.... This poor man cried, and the Lord heard him, and saved him out of all his troubles." David could still praise God in spite of the circumstances he was facing in exile. In Psalm 142:1 he said, "I cried unto the Lord with my voice; with my voice unto the Lord did I make my supplication." Psalm 31:1 says, "In thee, O Lord, do I put my trust; let me never be ashamed. Deliver me in thy righteousness." And in Psalm 7:1 he said, "O Lord my God, in thee do I put my trust; save me from all those who persecute me, and deliver me." David confidently trusted the Lord to protect him from Saul. What David experienced brought out the best in him, but it brought out the worst in Saul.

Love can turn to hatred and even to murder

when pride poisons our heart and envy controls our actions. No wonder Proverbs 4:23 warns us: "Keep thy heart with all diligence; for out of it are the issues of life."

Chapter 9

The Ultimate Weapon
(I Sam. 24,26)

On two different occasions David had the opportunity to kill King Saul. From a human point of view, Saul's death would have solved many problems. But David looked at life from *God's* point of view, not from the human perspective. On both of these occasions, three opportunities presented themselves. David faced an opportunity for *revenge* or for *restraint*, while Saul faced an opportunity for *repentance*. In I Samuel 24 David faced these choices in a cave, and in chapter 26 he faced them in the camp of Saul.

Temptation in the Cave

Let's begin with David's *temptation in the cave*. David and his men were in a cave in the wilderness of En-gedi. This is a terrible wilderness, dry and desolate, with many caves. Saul was there with 3000 chosen men, looking for David. He entered the cave in which David and his men were hiding but could not see them. The bright desert sun may have temporarily blinded him. Or David's men could have been hiding in the darkness so that Saul didn't know they were there.

"And the men of David said unto him, Behold, the day of which the Lord said unto thee, Behold, I will deliver thine enemy into thine hand, that thou mayest do to him as it shall seem good unto thee. Then David arose, and cut off the skirt of Saul's robe stealthily. And it came to pass afterward, that David's heart smote him, because he had cut off Saul's skirt. And he said unto his men, The Lord forbid that I should do this thing unto my master, the Lord's anointed, to stretch forth mine hand against him, seeing he is the anointed of the Lord. So David restrained his servants with these words" (I Sam. 24:4-7).

After Saul left the cave, David went out and called out to him: "My lord, the king. And when Saul looked behind him, David stooped with his face to the earth, and bowed himself. And David said to Saul, Why hearest thou men's words, saying, Behold, David seeketh thy harm? Behold, this day thine eyes have seen how that the Lord had delivered thee today into mine hand in the cave; and some bade me kill thee, but mine eye spared thee, and I said, I will not put forth mine hand against my lord; for he is the Lord's anointed" (vv. 8-10).

David had an opportunity for revenge, which seemed providential. David was encouraged by his friends to kill King Saul. In fact, they even argued that the word of the Lord permitted David to do it. After all, Samuel had said that God had rejected Saul (15:26), and Jonathan had said that the Lord
74

would cut off the enemies of David (20:15). Either of these statements would have given David the right to kill the king—at least in his friends' estimation. David did not yield to this temptation because he realized that Saul was not his enemy. David might have been Saul's enemy, but Saul was not David's enemy.

Some Bibles note that Psalm 18 was written when God delivered David from "the hand of all his enemies and from the hand of Saul." It's interesting that Saul is not classified among David's enemies.

Yes, David had an opportunity for revenge, but he also had an opportunity for restraint. Instead of taking revenge on Saul, David chose to restrain himself and his men, proving what a great man he was. Proverbs 16:32 says, "He who is slow to anger is better than the mighty; and he who ruleth his spirit, than he that taketh a city." David proved that he was truly a king by ruling and reigning over his own emotions. If he hadn't controlled his emotions, he might have reasoned as his friends did and rationalized that the situation was providential. He would have killed Saul rather than doing what was right.

Sometimes we think that God is giving us an opportunity to do things our own way. It looks as if He has arranged the opportunity, and perhaps even our best friends can give us biblical reasons for doing the wrong thing. We must be careful not to convince ourselves that what we want is really God's will for us when it isn't. We need to seek the Lord's will for our lives through prayer and Bible

75

study rather than allowing our emotions to control us.

What kept David from taking revenge against Saul? For one thing he respected Saul's authority. He called him "my master . . . the anointed of the Lord" (I Sam. 24:6). He also called him "the king" (v. 8) and "my father" (v. 11). (David was son-in-law to the king.) David respected the fact that Saul was God's anointed. He said, "I will not stretch forth my hand against the anointed of the Lord" (see v. 6).

David also had a very sensitive conscience. In fact, David regretted that he had cut off part of Saul's garment. Saul had laid aside his robe, and David secretly crept up and cut off a corner. He wanted to prove to Saul that he truly was there and could have slain him. But David's conscience rebuked him. David had a tender conscience that convicted him whenever he did something wrong.

David was very humble, and this also restrained him. "After whom is the king of Israel come out? After whom dost thou pursue? After a dead dog! After a flea!" (v. 14). In other words, David was saying, "I am nobody. Why are you chasing me?"

But the main reason David restrained himself was because he had faith in God. He said, "The Lord, therefore, be judge, and judge between me and thee, and see, and plead my cause, and deliver me out of thine hand" (v. 15). David had committed himself to the Righteous Judge, the One who would work all things together for good.

David took the opportunity for restraint because he was a godly man with integrity. For Saul, this situation presented him with an *opportunity for repentance*. This would have been the perfect opportunity for Saul to apologize to David, to repent of his sin and to let God work things out according to His will. Saul wept, but I don't think that these tears were sincere. He said to David, "Thou art more righteous than I; for thou hast rewarded me good, whereas I have rewarded thee evil" (v. 17). He added, "For if a man find his enemy, will he let him go well away? Wherefore, the Lord reward thee with good for what thou hast done unto me this day" (v. 19).

Saul's comments to David point out that there are three levels of life. There's the human level, where you return evil for evil (v. 19). If a man finds his enemy, he fights him. There is also the satanic level, where you return evil for good. That's where Saul was living: "I have rewarded thee evil" (v. 17). But David was living on the divine level, where you return good for evil. "For thou hast rewarded me good," said Saul (v. 17). This is the level on which we should live.

Saul did not repent but was only concerned about his family and his name. "Swear now, therefore, unto me by the Lord, that thou wilt not cut off my seed after me, and that thou wilt not destroy my name out of my father's house" (v. 21). Saul was a proud man, concerned only about his reputation.

David was living by a principle that Paul later stated in Romans 12:17-21: "Recompense to no man evil for evil. Provide things honest in the sight of all men. If it be possible, as much as lieth in you,

77

live peaceably with all men. Dearly beloved, avenge not yourselves but, rather, give place unto wrath [the wrath of God]; for it is written, Vengeance is mine; I will repay, saith the Lord. Therefore, if thine enemy hunger, feed him; if he thirst, give him drink; for in so doing thou shalt heap coals of fire on his head. Be not overcome by evil, but overcome evil with good."

Temptation in the Camp

In I Samuel 26 we have the account of the *temptation in the camp*. David sent his spies out and discovered that Saul was encamped nearby, so David and his nephew Abishai secretly entered the camp. God had caused a heavy sleep to come upon Saul and his soldiers. Once again, David was given an opportunity for revenge. As Saul lay sleeping, Abishai said to David, "God hath delivered thine enemy into thine hand this day" (v. 8). Saul's spear was there, the same spear that he had used more than once to try to kill David. If David had wanted revenge, what better weapon could he have used than the one that had been aimed at him?

But David said to Abishai, "Destroy him not; for who can stretch forth his hand against the Lord's anointed, and be guiltless?" (v. 9). Abishai had told him, in effect, "God has given you another chance, David! He has even put everyone to sleep! This is His doing—don't waste it!" But David understood that you can't know the will of God simply by circumstances. You must know the Word of God.

David knew it was wrong to kill the king of Israel,

78

so he did the next best thing: He took Saul's spear and his cruse of water. Then he and Abishai went outside the camp where they could be heard but not seen or caught. There David called to Abner, woke him up and said, "What kind of a bodyguard are you? I have Saul's spear and cruse of water. I could easily have killed the king. You deserve to die for not protecting him!" (see vv. 14-16). David would not humiliate Saul. He had done that when he cut off part of Saul's robe. But David did humiliate Abner, Saul's bodyguard.

Here was an opportunity for revenge, but David refused to accept it. He chose instead to restrain himself. David said, "As the Lord liveth, the Lord shall smite him; or his day shall come to die; or he shall descend into battle, and perish" (v. 10). David trusted God to punish Saul. He refused to take matters into his own hands.

Once again, God gave Saul an opportunity to repent. David said to Saul, "Now, therefore, I pray thee, let my lord, the king, hear the words of his servant. If the Lord have stirred thee up against me, let him accept an offering; but if they be the children of men, cursed be they before the Lord; for they have driven me out this day from abiding in the inheritance of the Lord, saying, Go, serve other gods" (v. 19). David made it clear that the people were creating this problem, not him, and that the king was listening to the slander and the malicious lies of some of the flatterers in his court.

When you read the 20 psalms that David wrote during his exile, you often read about "flattering

79

lips" and people who slandered David and lied about him. Saul believed these flatterers, but David warned, "God will punish those who have unjustly accused me. If you have sinned against the Lord, why don't you confess your sin? If you do this, He will then forgive and restore you."

Saul had lost his crown and his kingship, but he still could have ended his days in the will of God and at peace with David. Saul did not repent when he said, "I have sinned" (v. 21). I don't think he really meant these words. Neither did he mean it when he said, "I have played the fool, and have erred exceedingly" (v. 21). This was his opportunity for repentance, but he was not genuinely sorry for his sin. Instead, Saul continued to fight David and the Lord.

A man *does* "play the fool" when he sins and thinks he can get away with it. He plays the fool when he rebels against God and will not submit to Him. When Saul said, "I have sinned . . . I have played the fool" (v. 21), he was telling the truth, but he was not repenting.

A person also plays the fool when he rejects his good friends. David wanted to be Saul's friend. Samuel was Saul's friend, and yet Saul did nothing but create problems for Samuel. Yes, a person is a fool when he nurtures envy and hatred and refuses to repent. Saul's tears were evidence more of remorse than of repentance, for he did not humble himself before the Lord.

On two occasions David was given an opportunity for revenge or restraint, and Saul was given an opportunity for repentance. David chose to obey

God and restrained his desire for revenge. Saul chose to reject his opportunities for repentance and instead followed his own desires.

Saul used his spear and his army to fight David. However, David chose to use the weapons of love and forgiveness. David chose God's weapons and attained victory; Saul used powerful earthly weapons, but still he failed.

The ultimate weapon is love. Our task is to obey God and leave revenge to Him. Don't fight people— let God take care of your battles with others. We must fight sin and all that is evil, but we must not carry personal grudges. The best way to get rid of an enemy is to make him a friend.

David did everything he could to change Saul's attitude toward him. He was obeying Romans 12:18: "If it be possible, as much as lieth in you, live peaceably with all men." Sometimes it isn't possible. In David's case it wasn't possible because Saul would not surrender to the Lord.

I trust that you and I will learn to use God's ultimate weapon—love. Don't have enemies in your life. Don't fight back when people hurt you. Instead, forgive them. You are only hurting yourself when you play the fool and fight against those who are making life difficult for you. Surrender your desire for revenge to the Lord. "Vengeance is mine; I will repay, saith the Lord" (v. 19).

Chapter 10

A King in the Dark
(I Sam. 28)

The late president of the Moody Bible Institute in Chicago, William Culbertson, often prayed, "Lord help us to end well." The saintly British preacher, Dr. F. B. Meyer, said at the close of his life, "I don't want my life to end in a swamp."

Good beginnings are no guarantee of successful endings. King Saul is proof of that. If any man had a great opportunity for doing God's will, it was Saul. Yet King Saul ended up consulting a witch and then committing suicide on the battlefield.

"And it came to pass in those days, that the Philistines gathered their armies together for warfare, to fight with Israel" (I Sam. 28:1). This was *the* decisive battle. The Philistines were tired of little skirmishes, and they were determined to defeat Saul and Israel once and for all.

"Now Samuel was dead, and all Israel had lamented him, and buried him in Ramah, even in his own city. And Saul had put away those who were mediums, and the wizards, out of the land. . . . And when Saul saw the host of the Philistines, he was afraid, and his heart greatly trembled. And when

Saul inquired of the Lord, the Lord answered him not, neither by dreams, nor by Urim, nor by prophets. Then said Saul unto his servants, Seek me a woman who is a medium, that I may go to her, and inquire of her. And his servants said to him, Behold, there is a woman who is a medium at En-dor. And Saul disguised himself, and put on other raiment, and he went, and two men with him, and they came to the woman by night; and he said, I pray thee, divine unto me as a medium, and bring me him up, whom I shall name unto thee" (vv. 3,5-8).

The Scriptures tell us that Saul "disguised himself." In one sense, Saul was *revealing* himself! The darkness in his soul was coming out. In order to get from Gilboa to En-dor, Saul had to travel 10 or 12 miles and had to pass near the enemy camp. Saul risked his life in disguising himself and making that trip, but he was a desperate man. God had forsaken him.

Saul told the witch at En-dor that he wanted to talk to Samuel. Ordinarily, she would have been used by a demon, and the demon would have impersonated Samuel. But this time, God permitted Samuel to come back! The woman was surprised when she saw Samuel because she had not been responsible for his appearance! She realized that God was at work.

Saul told Samuel how distressed he was because God had departed from him and because he didn't know what to do. Samuel replied, in effect, "I told you so. I warned you, but you wouldn't listen. You did not obey the will of the Lord. You rebelled against Him, and now judgment is coming." Samuel issued a warning: "Moreover, the Lord will also deliver Israel with thee into the hand of the Philistines, and tomorrow shalt thou and thy sons be with me [in the realm of the dead]. The Lord also shall deliver the host of Israel into the hand of the Philistines. Then Saul fell immediately full length on the earth, and was very much afraid, because of the words of Samuel; and there was no strength in him; for he had eaten no bread all the day, nor all the night" (vv. 19,20).

It is dangerous to rebel against the will of God. When you see the contrast between Saul's beginning and his ending, you can see how important it is to obey the will of God. Let's look at these contrasts.

Light Versus Darkness

In the beginning, Saul was in the *light*; but at the end, he was in *darkness*. When Saul was anointed king, it was dawn. "And they [Samuel and Saul] arose early; and it came to pass about the dawn of the day, that Samuel called Saul to the top of the house, saying, Up, that I may send thee away. And Saul arose, and they went out both of them, he and Samuel, abroad. And as they were going down to the end of the city, Samuel said to Saul, Bid the servant pass on before us (and he passed on), but stand thou still a while, that I may show thee the word of God" (I Sam. 9:26,27).

At the beginning of Saul's reign, we see him in the

light. Saul was anointed at the "dawn of the day." It was also the dawning of a new day in his life. God gave Saul everything he needed for success—an endowment of power and a group of men whose hearts He had touched—when he was anointed. But when you turn to I Samuel 28, you don't find any sign of dawn. You find darkness! Saul disguised himself and went to the witch by night. "For everyone that doeth evil hateth the light, neither cometh to the light, lest his deeds should be reproved" (John 3:20).

In the Bible darkness is a picture of sin. "God is light, and in him is no darkness at all" (I John 1:5). Satan is the prince of darkness. When Saul and his two friends left for En-dor, it was still night. Saul began his kingship in the light, but he ended it in the darkness. Why? Because he rebelled against the will of God.

Courage Versus Fear

The second contrast is a contrast between *courage* and *fear*. At the beginning of Saul's reign, he was a great man of courage. When the Ammonites invaded and word came to Saul that the people were weeping, Saul cut up an oxen, distributed the parts and said, "Everybody follow me!" With great courage, he went to battle and defeated the enemy. But at our present point in the story, Saul is trembling and afraid as he sees the host of the Philistines.

It's interesting to note the growing fear in Saul's life. In I Samuel 12, when the kingdom was established at Gilgal, Samuel warned Saul to fear God.

86

"Only fear the Lord, and serve him in truth with all your heart" (v. 24). But Saul did not have a wholehearted commitment to the Lord. He was told to fear the Lord, but in chapter 15 he started to fear the people. Then in chapter 18 he feared David and became envious and filled with hatred. In chapter 28, when Saul saw the host of the Philistines, he was greatly afraid and his heart trembled.

Courage comes from a pure heart. When your conscience is right with God, you have courage. Proverbs 28:1 says, "The wicked flee when no man pursueth, but the righteous are bold as a lion." David knew that he could have victory because his heart was right with God. Saul was facing defeat because his heart was not right with God.

Wisdom Versus Folly

A third contrast in this passage is the one between *wisdom* and *folly*. In the beginning Saul used wisdom, but in the end he practiced folly. Saul began his rule by listening to the wisdom of God. He went to Gilgal and listened to Samuel review God's mighty works for Israel. He listened to the Word of God. Samuel told him what to do, and Saul did it. Initially he sought the wisdom of the Lord, but gradually he became a fool.

God's people should walk in His wisdom and not in the foolishness of man. We have the Holy Spirit to guide us so that we can obey the will of the Lord. It's a tragedy when a person tries to live his own life his own way according to his own will. The Word of

God says in Ephesians 5:17, "Wherefore, be ye not unwise but understanding what the will of the Lord is." How do you understand what the will of the Lord is? By being filled with the Holy Spirit.

The tragedy for Saul was that the Spirit of God had *departed from him!* As a result, Saul acted like a fool. He disobeyed the Word of God, made excuses and lied. He blamed others—Samuel, Jonathan, the people—everyone but himself. When Saul desperately needed to know what to do, he inquired of the Lord, but the Lord did not answer him. The priest was not able to use the Urim to determine the will of God. The prophets had no word for him. He had no direction from God, so he stooped to folly. It was as if Saul said, "If I can't find out what God wants me to do in the usual ways, I'll go to a witch and see if she can help me. I need to talk to Samuel."

Isn't it a tragedy that Saul realized too late how much he needed Samuel? He had ignored Samuel when he was there to help. When Samuel had prayed for Saul, Saul didn't care. When Samuel had given Saul direction, Saul did not listen. Now when he realized how valuable Samuel was, he could no longer turn to him for help. Samuel wasn't there to pray for him or to give him guidance because he had died. Saul had rejected his best friend.

Do you have someone—a pastor, a parent, a friend—who wants to guide you in the right direction, but you aren't paying any attention? I want to warn you: One day that person may be gone, and you will wish you had his or her wisdom. Appreciate the people who try to help you!

Standing Versus Falling

The fourth contrast is one between *standing* and *falling.* Saul began his career standing, but he ended it falling. I have pointed out in these studies how Saul changed his posture as he declined in his spiritual life. We saw that when Saul became king, he was not only tall in stature but was also admired by the people. But then King Saul rebelled against the Lord, and God rejected him as king. First, Saul was *standing;* then he was *walking;* but when he turned his back on God, he began *falling!*

Saul began his reign with such great prospects and such tremendous potential, but he fell both physically and spiritually because of his pride. "Then Saul fell immediately full length on the earth, and was very much afraid" (I Sam. 28:20). The once proud king is prostrate on the earth! He falls again on the battlefield (31:4). He fell on his sword and committed suicide. The king who refused to humble himself before God ends his life in humiliation, stripped of his pride.

When David received word that Saul and Jonathan were dead, he sang a lamentation (II Sam. 1). Three times David said, "How are the mighty fallen!" (vv. 19,25,27). He was referring to their death on the battlefield, but I think there is a spiritual lesson in those words. Saul had fallen spiritually long before he fell in death.

Victory Versus Defeat

The fifth and final contrast is between *victory* and *defeat.* Saul began his kingship with victory—

89

victory over the enemy and over his own spirit. He was able to control his temper and did not retaliate. But when we get to the end of his life, we see him in tragic defeat.

I suppose no battle listed in the Bible is filled with more shame and tragedy than the battle of Gilboa where Saul and Jonathan and the army were defeated by their enemies, the Philistines. Saul knew he was going to die; and in a sense, he showed great courage. He knew he was going to lose the battle; he knew he and his sons were going to die, and yet he went courageously into battle and did his best. But his best was not enough. God had deserted him, and he could only fail. Saul fell on his sword and committed suicide rather than dying at the hands of the Philistines.

Saul lost his kingship and his crown, but I think God would have forgiven and restored him if Saul had truly repented. Saul could have had a more noble death, but he rejected the will of the Lord and rebelled against the word of the Lord. He ended up dying a tragic, shameful death on the battlefield.

A good beginning is no guarantee of a successful ending. We must pray as Dr. Culbertson used to pray, "Lord, help us to end well." Our opportunity for confession, for repentance, for restitution may be gone tomorrow; we need to take advantage of it today.

It's possible for us to start in light and end in darkness, to begin our Christian life with great courage and end it in fear, to start out with God's wisdom and end up in human folly, to begin by

90

standing and end by falling. It's possible to start with great victory and end in defeat. Unlike Saul, David realized how easy it is to fall and how much he needed the Lord's help. No wonder he prayed after he sinned with Bathsheba, "Create in me a clean heart, O God, and renew a right spirit within me" (Ps. 51:10).

May the Lord help us to end well!

Chapter 11

The King Is Dead!
(I Sam. 31; II Sam. 1)

If we were to flash on the screen the closing scenes of King Saul's life, we would see four vivid pictures entitled: defeat, death, disgrace and devotion. These scenes are found in I Samuel 31 and II Samuel 1. Defeat, death, disgrace and devotion—these same four words could describe our lives. "Let him that thinketh he standeth take heed lest he fall" (I Cor. 10:12).

Defeat

In I Samuel 31:1,2 we find the first picture entitled *defeat*: "Now the Philistines fought against Israel; and the men of Israel fled from before the Philistines, and fell down slain in Mount Gilboa. And the Philistines followed hard upon Saul and upon his sons; and the Philistines slew Jonathan, and Abinadab, and Malchi-shua, Saul's sons."

The word that best describes this picture is *defeat*. The army is fleeing and falling, and the enemy is winning. Saul started his career with great victory, but he gradually began to move down the path that leads to defeat. He is now *fleeing*. Why is

93

he fleeing? Because he now knows that he has no one to blame but himself. He began to realize this the night before when he talked to Samuel, whom God permitted to come back from the dead. Samuel reminded Saul of his disobedience and told him, "Tomorrow you are going to be where I am—in the world of the dead" (see 28:15-19).

Saul's whole problem was that he fought the wrong enemy. He thought David was his enemy when, in reality, Saul was his own worst enemy. David never treated Saul like an enemy, but Saul chased David all over the wilderness of Judea, trying to slay him. Saul should have been out fighting the real enemy, the Philistines, and yet he was fighting David instead. Samuel told Saul, "Why, then, dost thou ask of me, seeing the Lord is departed from thee, and is become thine enemy?" (v. 16). Saul fought the wrong enemy, so God had to discipline him. "The carnal mind is enmity against God" (Rom. 8:7). Saul was his own worst enemy because he disobeyed God and rebelled against His will.

As you witness the end of Saul's life, you see a man who is *fleeing* and *falling*. This is tragic because God had given Saul great promises and great prospects. Saul had a good friend in Samuel, a capable associate in Jonathan and a faithful helper in David. He had a band of loyal followers. He was endowed with power from the Holy Spirit, and he had natural gifts that God could use. And yet Saul was defeated on the battlefield of Mount Gilboa.

Where does defeat come from? Defeat comes from the *inside*, not from the *outside*. It is always a
94

problem of the heart. "Keep thy heart with all diligence; for out of it are the issues of life" (Prov. 4:23). Saul was defeated in his spiritual life. This is why he was defeated in his military life.

Death

The second picture at the end of Saul's life can be entitled *death*. "And the battle went heavily against Saul, and the archers hit him; and he was severely wounded by the archers. Then said Saul unto his armor-bearer, Draw thy sword, and thrust me through with it, lest these uncircumcised come and thrust me through, and abuse me. But his armor-bearer would not; for he was very much afraid. Therefore Saul took a sword, and fell upon it. And when his armor-bearer saw that Saul was dead, he fell likewise upon his sword, and died with him. So Saul died, and his three sons, and his armor-bearer, and all his men that same day together" (I Sam. 31:3-6).

Verse 6 does not mean that the entire army died that day. "All his men" refers to all the royal body-guard. You will recall that, at one point, David had been Saul's armor-bearer. If David had not separated from Saul, he might have been in that battle and died. How marvelous are the ways of the Lord! David could not understand why all those difficulties happened to him, but in the end those trials spared his life and enabled him to be the great king of Israel.

Defeat leads to death. How sad it is to see Israel's first king dying in shame from committing suicide on

95

the battlefield. From a military point of view, this may have been a great act of courage. Saul did not want the enemy to take him alive, abuse him and torture him. They would have done to him what they did to Samson, and Saul didn't want that. He would rather die than be captured, so he committed suicide. Then his armor-bearer committed suicide.

What a tragedy that others had to die with Saul! Jonathan was slain—a man of faith and courage, a great warrior and David's dear friend. David and Jonathan had loved one another affectionately and had encouraged one another. All of Saul's sons died with their father in the battle. "The wages of sin is death" (Rom. 6:23). "There is a sin unto death" (I John 5:16). "So Saul died for his trangression which he committed against the Lord, even against the word of the Lord, which he kept not, and also for asking counsel of a medium, to inquire of her, and inquired not of the Lord; therefore, he slew him, and turned the kingdom unto David, the son of Jesse" (I Chron. 10:13,14).

Throughout his career Saul transgressed against God's Word and disobeyed His will. God told him to wait, but he ran ahead. God told him to fight, but he lingered. God told him to destroy the Amalekites, but he spared Agag the king and the best of the spoil. These actions may not seem like great sins to us, but they were contrary to the will of God; and anything we do that is contrary to the will of God is serious. That is why Saul died.

Our God is patient. He does not suddenly send judgment. How patient He was with King Saul, and yet Saul did not use the opportunities he was given for repentance. He ignored his chances to make things right with David and with the Lord. Therefore, he died a shameful death. It's dangerous to rebel against the will of God.

Disgrace

The third picture is one of *disgrace*. "And when the men of Israel who were on the other side of the valley, and they who were on the other side of the Jordan, saw that the men of Israel fled, and that Saul and his sons were dead, they forsook the cities, and fled; and the Philistines came and dwelt in them. And it came to pass on the next day, when the Philistines came to strip the slain, that they found Saul and his three sons fallen in Mount Gilboa. And they cut off his head, and stripped off his armor, and sent into the land of the Philistines round about, to publish it in the house of their idols, and among the people. And they put his armor in the house of Ashtaroth; and they fastened his body to the wall of Beth-shan" (I Sam. 31:7-10).

What a disgraceful end for the king of Israel! The nation had fled in panic. The bodies of the royal family were abused and exposed publicly in disgrace. Can't you hear the Philistines jeering and saying, "This was the great King Saul"? Worse than that the name of the Lord was blasphemed. The enemy took Saul's armor to the house of their idols and gave glory to their false gods for the victory they had won. That's the tragic result of disobedience: It gives ammunition to the enemy so he can blas-

97

pheme the Lord and bring disgrace on God's people.

Devotion

The story doesn't end on a negative note however. The fourth picture is one of *devotion*. The men of Jabesh-gilead heard what had happened to Saul, and they courageously traveled all night into enemy territory to rescue the bodies of Saul and his three sons. Saul had once rescued the people of Jabesh-gilead (I Sam. 11:1-11). Now in appreciation for what Saul had done for them, they came and gave these bodies proper burial and honor.

We need to remember that Saul had done some good things. I've had to conduct funeral services for people who apparently were very wicked, but someone could always remember something good the person had done. Though Saul had fallen morally and spiritually, the men of Jabesh-gilead said, in effect, "We owe our lives to him, and we're going to treat him the way he ought to be treated." Some years later David reburied these bodies in the land that belonged to the tribe of Benjamin so Saul would be with his own people.

Not only did the men of Jabesh-gilead show devotion to Saul, but David also showed devotion. In II Samuel 1 an Amalekite ran into David's camp and told David how the battle had turned out. He reported that the enemy had won and that Saul and his sons were dead. Then he told how he had helped to kill Saul. I think the Amalekite made this story up, hoping to win a reward from David. He claimed that Saul had asked him to kill him because he had tried to kill himself but had failed. The Amalekite said, "So I stood over him, and slew him, because I was sure that he could not live after he was fallen. And I took the crown that was upon his head, and the bracelet that was on his arm, and have brought them here unto my lord" (v. 10). This Amalekite thought he was going to receive favors from David, but he did not realize that Saul was not David's enemy.

David showed his devotion to Saul and Jonathan in several ways. To begin with, David defended Saul's honor by executing the Amalekite. He said, "How could you destroy the anointed of the Lord?" (see v. 14). He defended Saul's honor and then mourned his death. David and his men spent the rest of the day fasting and weeping as they mourned the death of Saul and Jonathan.

David wrote a beautiful song called "The Song of the Bow" (vv. 18-27). Note the refrain that is repeated three times: "How are the mighty fallen!" (vv. 19,25,27). Throughout this song, you don't find David uttering one negative word about Saul. He called him the glory of Israel (see v. 19), a mighty man (see v. 21) and the anointed of Israel (see v. 21). David sang of Saul's victorious sword (see v. 22). "Saul and Jonathan were lovely and pleasant in their lives, and in their death they were not divided; they were swifter than eagles, they were stronger than lions" (v. 23). In this song David gave honor and glory to the Lord for what Saul had done. He also added a special word of lament for Jonathan, his dear friend (see vv. 25,26).

David forgave Saul and honored him. He did not stand up and say, "Let me tell you what a scoundrel Saul was!" No, David was a man after God's own heart. God forgives and forgets, and David was also forgiving. David did not mention Saul's rebellion or the fact that Saul had tried to kill him. David honored Saul as king, even though Saul had lost his life and his crown.

I think that the saddest statement is in verse 10: "And I took the crown." This reminds me of Revelation 3:11: "Behold, I come quickly; hold that fast which thou hast, that no man take thy crown." Saul lost his crown. Let's be faithful to God so we don't lose our crown.

Chapter 12

Lessons Saul Never Learned

The biographies of the great men and women in the Bible were written for our encouragement and for our warning. "For whatever things were written in earlier times were written for our learning, that we, through patience and comfort of the scriptures, might have hope" (Rom. 15:4). First Corinthians 10:11 tells us, "Now all these things happened unto them for examples, and they are written for our admonition, upon whom the ends of the ages are come." It isn't necessary for us to learn the hard way. We can learn from the mistakes of others, even from the mistakes of people such as King Saul.

As we have studied the life of King Saul, we have discovered that there were many lessons Saul did not learn. There is no reason why you and I should disobey the Lord and learn these lessons the hard way. Let's learn instead from King Saul. What lessons can you and I learn today from Saul's life that will encourage us to serve the Lord, obey His will and glorify His name? I have made a list of five fundamental lessons that I have learned from the life of King Saul. We need to learn and apply these lessons so that we obey the Lord and do not lose our crown.

Sin Is Serious

The first lesson we can learn is that *sin is serious.* One of Saul's problems was that he did not take sin seriously but treated it lightly. What are the evidences in Saul's life that show this? Saul always made excuses instead of confessing his sin. He was quick to blame other people for what he himself had done. He blamed Samuel when he did not arrive at the appointed time. Saul ran ahead of the will of God, but he blamed Samuel for it. He blamed Jonathan, and he also blamed the people. When Samuel rebuked Saul for sparing Agag and the spoil from the Amalekites, Saul said, "The people did this."

Sin is serious, but you never find Saul truly repenting. You find him weeping when David spared his life, and he even said, "I have sinned! I have played the fool!" But you never find Saul really brokenhearted, confessing his sin to the Lord.

From a human point of view, David was guilty of sins that seemed much more serious than those Saul committed. All sin is serious, but some sins seem worse than others. Saul was impatient and ran ahead of God's will. He was also stubborn and lagged behind God's will. But David committed adultery! He made a man drunk and then had him murdered! One day, David gave the order to number all of the people to show how great he was; and as a result, 70 thousand people died! But whenever David sinned, he confessed his sins to God. He had a broken heart before God because he was a man after God's own heart. God forgave and restored David. Yes, David was disciplined and chastened for his sins, but he did not lose his crown.

The first lesson we need to learn from Saul's life is that sin is serious. We may think that we can cover up our sins, but eventually they will be revealed.

Spiritual Decline Is Gradual

The second lesson is this: *Spiritual decline is gradual.* Saul's failure was not immediate. Saul began by standing and walking, but after he turned away from the Lord, he began to fall. At first Saul was humble, but soon pride came in and, with pride came envy. He envied David's success and popularity. Hatred followed envy, and murder followed hatred. Gradually Saul declined in his spiritual life. At first he was obedient, but then he started making excuses, scheming and plotting. He rebelled against God and decided to go his own way. He began his reign by being very cooperative with both Samuel and David. He even loved David. But then, little by little, he became stubborn and independent, and he lost his two good friends.

Spiritual decline is gradual. It's possible for our spiritual life to deteriorate without our really knowing it. It's possible for our spiritual fervor to change so gradually that we can't detect it. Others may not be able to detect it either. Spiritual decline can be so gradual that before we know it, we have fallen.

Integrity Is Essential

A third lesson comes to us from the life of Saul: *Integrity is essential.* Saul was a double-minded

103

man, and the Word of God tells us, "A double minded man is unstable in all his ways" (James 1:8). At the beginning of his reign, Saul *served God* (I Sam. 11,12). He did what God wanted him to do. Then quietly he began to *serve God and himself.* He was using his opportunities to get what *he* wanted. Finally, Saul started *using God to serve him* (I Sam. 15). God commanded him to completely destroy the Amalekites, but Saul decided he wanted something for himself out of this battle. He used God to serve himself. As a result, Saul was abandoned by God, the Holy Spirit was taken from him, and he was left alone. He prayed, but he received no answer. He sought God's guidance, but no direction came. Saul lacked integrity. He was trying to serve two masters—God and himself.

David was known for his integrity of heart. This is why God called him: "He chose David his servant, and took him from the sheepfolds; from following the ewes great with young, he brought him to feed Jacob, his people, and Israel, his inheritance. So he fed them according to the integrity of his heart, and guided them by the skillfulness of his hands" (Ps. 78:70-72). Saul had skillful hands. He could throw a spear and wield a sword. He was a skilled archer. Saul had skillful hands, but he did not have integrity of heart. His heart was divided. He attempted to serve both God and himself.

Singlehearted devotion to God is so important. "No servant can serve two masters; for either he will hate the one, and love the other; or else he will hold to the one, and despise the other" (Luke

16:13). You cannot look in two directions at the same time. "The lamp of the body is the eye; therefore, when thine eye is sound, thy whole body also is full of light; but when thine eye is evil, thy body also is full of darkness" (11:34). This is what happened to Saul. He ended up in the darkness because he was a double-minded man.

Obedience Is the Key to Victory and Success

The fourth lesson is that *obedience is the key to victory and success.* God must be the Lord of our lives. God made Saul the king. He anointed him and empowered him. Yet He was not in control of Saul's life because Saul did not allow Him to have control.

We must make God's will our will. We must not argue with God, rebel against Him, run ahead of Him or lag behind Him. When God tells us what to do, we must do it. "Be not conformed to this world, but be ye transformed by the renewing of your mind, that ye may prove what is that good, and acceptable, and perfect, will of God" (Rom. 12:2). This refers to living by faith. God doesn't have to give us a reason for everything He asks us to do. When He tells us what to do, our task is to obey without question.

Sacrifice is no substitute for obedience. We may think, *Well, I tithe and give generously to missions; therefore, I can get away with sin.* God does not want our sacrifices. The only sacrifice He wants is an obedient heart. "A broken and a contrite heart, O God, thou wilt not despise" (Ps. 51:17).

We Must Build Our Spiritual Lives

We can learn a fifth lesson from Saul: *We must build our spiritual lives or we will fall.* It's interesting that you don't find Saul building anything. One day he put up a monument to celebrate his victory over the Amalekites, but it was actually a monument to his spiritual defeat.

David was always building his spiritual life. When you read about his life and read the psalms he wrote, you see a man who was constantly growing in his spiritual life and in his knowledge of God. He was growing in his prayer life and in his understanding of God's truth. Saul was good at fighting battles and making enemies, but you don't find him building anything. One day he started to build an altar, but he never finished it. If we don't build our spiritual lives, we are going to fall.

I think Saul depended on his natural gifts. He may have thought, *I'm the first king, and God has anointed me. I'm a great warrior and a good leader. I stand head and shoulders above everyone else. Therefore, I am going to succeed.* But he did not succeed because he did not build his spiritual life.

Jude talked about this in his letter: "But ye, beloved, building up yourselves on your most holy faith, praying in the Holy Spirit" (1:20). Saul did not live by faith. Instead, he walked by sight. He saw the enemy and feared. He saw the danger and fled. We don't find that Saul ever prayed. In fact, the Holy Spirit departed from him (I Sam. 16:14). Are you

106

building up your faith? Are you praying in the Holy Spirit?

"Keep yourselves in the love of God" (Jude 1:21). Saul did not keep himself in the love of God the way David did. When you love God, you keep His commandments. When you love God, you also love His people. Saul hated David. When he heard the women praising David's conquests, Saul was filled with envy and anger. Envy turned into hatred, and hatred led to murder. He tried to kill David. He even told his own son to kill David. Saul did not have love in his heart. He was not constrained by love; instead, he was driven by pride. His only concern was to have his own way.

"But ye, beloved, building up yourselves on your most holy faith, praying in the Holy Spirit, keep yourselves in the love of God, looking for the mercy of our Lord Jesus Christ unto eternal life" (vv. 20,21). We depend on God's mercy. But we are told in II Samuel 7:15 that God took His mercy away from Saul. Saul was not living in the will of God or experiencing the mercy of God. No wonder he fell!

Verse 24 of Jude 1 tells us the secret of victory: "Now unto him that is able to keep you from falling." God will do *His* part to keep us from falling if we will do *our* part. What is our part? Building ourselves up in our faith, praying in the Holy Spirit, keeping ourselves in the love of God and looking for the mercy of our Lord Jesus Christ. We must have *faith, hope* and *love*. We must obey God's Word and allow the Holy Spirit to teach us the truths of the Word.

Saul did not do these things. He was worldly, selfish and proud. He had tremendous opportunities, but he wasted them. He had valuable gifts, but he failed to use them.

"Now unto him that is able to keep you from falling, and to present you faultless before the presence of his glory with exceeding joy, to the only wise God, our Savior, be glory and majesty, dominion and power, both now and ever. Amen" (vv. 24,25). When you live for the glory of God, it makes a big difference in your life. Saul did not live for the glory of God but for the praise of men. He wanted to please the people. He was more concerned about his reputation than he was about his character.

We need to learn the lessons that Saul never learned: Sin is serious. Spiritual decline is gradual. Integrity is essential. Obedience is the key to victory and success. And most important of all, we must build our spiritual lives or we will fall. I remind you once again of the admonition from our Lord in Revelation 3:11: "Behold, I come quickly; hold that fast which thou hast, that no man take thy crown."

Don't lose your crown! Submit yourself to the Lord so that one day He can present you before God's throne and give you a crown of glory.